Mometrix
TEST PREPARATION

Certified Six Sigma Yellow Belt Exam Secrets Study Guide

Dear Future Exam Success Story

First of all, **THANK YOU** for purchasing Mometrix study materials!

Second, congratulations! You are one of the few determined test-takers who are committed to doing whatever it takes to excel on your exam. **You have come to the right place.** We developed these study materials with one goal in mind: to deliver you the information you need in a format that's concise and easy to use.

In addition to optimizing your guide for the content of the test, we've outlined our recommended steps for breaking down the preparation process into small, attainable goals so you can make sure you stay on track.

We've also analyzed the entire test-taking process, identifying the most common pitfalls and showing how you can overcome them and be ready for any curveball the test throws you.

Standardized testing is one of the biggest obstacles on your road to success, which only increases the importance of doing well in the high-pressure, high-stakes environment of test day. Your results on this test could have a significant impact on your future, and this guide provides the information and practical advice to help you achieve your full potential on test day.

Your success is our success

We would love to hear from you! If you would like to share the story of your exam success or if you have any questions or comments in regard to our products, please contact us at **800-673-8175** or **support@mometrix.com**.

Thanks again for your business and we wish you continued success!

Sincerely,
The Mometrix Test Preparation Team

Need more help? Check out our flashcards at:
http://MometrixFlashcards.com/SixSigma

Written and edited by the Mometrix Exam Secrets Test Prep Team
Printed in the United States of America

TABLE OF CONTENTS

Introduction

Thank you for purchasing this resource! You have made the choice to prepare yourself for a test that could have a huge impact on your future, and this guide is designed to help you be fully ready for test day. Obviously, it's important to have a solid understanding of the test material, but you also need to be prepared for the unique environment and stressors of the test, so that you can perform to the best of your abilities.

For this purpose, the first section that appears in this guide is the **Secret Keys**. We've devoted countless hours to meticulously researching what works and what doesn't, and we've boiled down our findings to the five most impactful steps you can take to improve your performance on the test. We start at the beginning with study planning and move through the preparation process, all the way to the testing strategies that will help you get the most out of what you know when you're finally sitting in front of the test.

We recommend that you start preparing for your test as far in advance as possible. However, if you've bought this guide as a last-minute study resource and only have a few days before your test, we recommend that you skip over the first two Secret Keys since they address a long-term study plan.

If you struggle with **test anxiety**, we strongly encourage you to check out our recommendations for how you can overcome it. Test anxiety is a formidable foe, but it can be beaten, and we want to make sure you have the tools you need to defeat it.

Secret Key #1 – Plan Big, Study Small

There's a lot riding on your performance. If you want to ace this test, you're going to need to keep your skills sharp and the material fresh in your mind. You need a plan that lets you review everything you need to know while still fitting in your schedule. We'll break this strategy down into three categories.

Information Organization

Start with the information you already have: the official test outline. From this, you can make a complete list of all the concepts you need to cover before the test. Organize these concepts into groups that can be studied together, and create a list of any related vocabulary you need to learn so you can brush up on any difficult terms. You'll want to keep this vocabulary list handy once you actually start studying since you may need to add to it along the way.

Time Management

Once you have your set of study concepts, decide how to spread them out over the time you have left before the test. Break your study plan into small, clear goals so you have a manageable task for each day and know exactly what you're doing. Then just focus on one small step at a time. When you manage your time this way, you don't need to spend hours at a time studying. Studying a small block of content for a short period each day helps you retain information better and avoid stressing over how much you have left to do. You can relax knowing that you have a plan to cover everything in time. In order for this strategy to be effective though, you have to start studying early and stick to your schedule. Avoid the exhaustion and futility that comes from last-minute cramming!

Study Environment

The environment you study in has a big impact on your learning. Studying in a coffee shop, while probably more enjoyable, is not likely to be as fruitful as studying in a quiet room. It's important to keep distractions to a minimum. You're only planning to study for a short block of time, so make the most of it. Don't pause to check your phone or get up to find a snack. It's also important to **avoid multitasking**. Research has consistently shown that multitasking will make your studying dramatically less effective. Your study area should also be comfortable and well-lit so you don't have the distraction of straining your eyes or sitting on an uncomfortable chair.

The time of day you study is also important. You want to be rested and alert. Don't wait until just before bedtime. Study when you'll be most likely to comprehend and remember. Even better, if you know what time of day your test will be, set that time aside for study. That way your brain will be used to working on that subject at that specific time and you'll have a better chance of recalling information.

Finally, it can be helpful to team up with others who are studying for the same test. Your actual studying should be done in as isolated an environment as possible, but the work of organizing the information and setting up the study plan can be divided up. In between study sessions, you can discuss with your teammates the concepts that you're all studying and quiz each other on the details. Just be sure that your teammates are as serious about the test as you are. If you find that your study time is being replaced with social time, you might need to find a new team.

Secret Key #2 – Make Your Studying Count

You're devoting a lot of time and effort to preparing for this test, so you want to be absolutely certain it will pay off. This means doing more than just reading the content and hoping you can remember it on test day. It's important to make every minute of study count. There are two main areas you can focus on to make your studying count.

Retention

It doesn't matter how much time you study if you can't remember the material. You need to make sure you are retaining the concepts. To check your retention of the information you're learning, try recalling it at later times with minimal prompting. Try carrying around flashcards and glance at one or two from time to time or ask a friend who's also studying for the test to quiz you.

To enhance your retention, look for ways to put the information into practice so that you can apply it rather than simply recalling it. If you're using the information in practical ways, it will be much easier to remember. Similarly, it helps to solidify a concept in your mind if you're not only reading it to yourself but also explaining it to someone else. Ask a friend to let you teach them about a concept you're a little shaky on (or speak aloud to an imaginary audience if necessary). As you try to summarize, define, give examples, and answer your friend's questions, you'll understand the concepts better and they will stay with you longer. Finally, step back for a big picture view and ask yourself how each piece of information fits with the whole subject. When you link the different concepts together and see them working together as a whole, it's easier to remember the individual components.

Finally, practice showing your work on any multi-step problems, even if you're just studying. Writing out each step you take to solve a problem will help solidify the process in your mind, and you'll be more likely to remember it during the test.

Modality

Modality simply refers to the means or method by which you study. Choosing a study modality that fits your own individual learning style is crucial. No two people learn best in exactly the same way, so it's important to know your strengths and use them to your advantage.

For example, if you learn best by visualization, focus on visualizing a concept in your mind and draw an image or a diagram. Try color-coding your notes, illustrating them, or creating symbols that will trigger your mind to recall a learned concept. If you learn best by hearing or discussing information, find a study partner who learns the same way or read aloud to yourself. Think about how to put the information in your own words. Imagine that you are giving a lecture on the topic and record yourself so you can listen to it later.

For any learning style, flashcards can be helpful. Organize the information so you can take advantage of spare moments to review. Underline key words or phrases. Use different colors for different categories. Mnemonic devices (such as creating a short list in which every item starts with the same letter) can also help with retention. Find what works best for you and use it to store the information in your mind most effectively and easily.

Secret Key #3 – Practice the Right Way

Your success on test day depends not only on how many hours you put into preparing, but also on whether you prepared the right way. It's good to check along the way to see if your studying is paying off. One of the most effective ways to do this is by taking practice tests to evaluate your progress. Practice tests are useful because they show exactly where you need to improve. Every time you take a practice test, pay special attention to these three groups of questions:

- The questions you got wrong
- The questions you had to guess on, even if you guessed right
- The questions you found difficult or slow to work through

This will show you exactly what your weak areas are, and where you need to devote more study time. Ask yourself why each of these questions gave you trouble. Was it because you didn't understand the material? Was it because you didn't remember the vocabulary? Do you need more repetitions on this type of question to build speed and confidence? Dig into those questions and figure out how you can strengthen your weak areas as you go back to review the material.

Additionally, many practice tests have a section explaining the answer choices. It can be tempting to read the explanation and think that you now have a good understanding of the concept. However, an explanation likely only covers part of the question's broader context. Even if the explanation makes perfect sense, **go back and investigate** every concept related to the question until you're positive you have a thorough understanding.

As you go along, keep in mind that the practice test is just that: practice. Memorizing these questions and answers will not be very helpful on the actual test because it is unlikely to have any of the same exact questions. If you only know the right answers to the sample questions, you won't be prepared for the real thing. **Study the concepts** until you understand them fully, and then you'll be able to answer any question that shows up on the test.

It's important to wait on the practice tests until you're ready. If you take a test on your first day of study, you may be overwhelmed by the amount of material covered and how much you need to learn. Work up to it gradually.

On test day, you'll need to be prepared for answering questions, managing your time, and using the test-taking strategies you've learned. It's a lot to balance, like a mental marathon that will have a big impact on your future. Like training for a marathon, you'll need to start slowly and work your way up. When test day arrives, you'll be ready.

Start with the strategies you've read in the first two Secret Keys—plan your course and study in the way that works best for you. If you have time, consider using multiple study resources to get different approaches to the same concepts. It can be helpful to see difficult concepts from more than one angle. Then find a good source for practice tests. Many times, the test website will suggest potential study resources or provide sample tests.

Practice Test Strategy

If you're able to find at least three practice tests, we recommend this strategy:

UNTIMED AND OPEN-BOOK PRACTICE

Take the first test with no time constraints and with your notes and study guide handy. Take your time and focus on applying the strategies you've learned.

TIMED AND OPEN-BOOK PRACTICE

Take the second practice test open-book as well, but set a timer and practice pacing yourself to finish in time.

TIMED AND CLOSED-BOOK PRACTICE

Take any other practice tests as if it were test day. Set a timer and put away your study materials. Sit at a table or desk in a quiet room, imagine yourself at the testing center, and answer questions as quickly and accurately as possible.

Keep repeating timed and closed-book tests on a regular basis until you run out of practice tests or it's time for the actual test. Your mind will be ready for the schedule and stress of test day, and you'll be able to focus on recalling the material you've learned.

Secret Key #4 – Pace Yourself

Once you're fully prepared for the material on the test, your biggest challenge on test day will be managing your time. Just knowing that the clock is ticking can make you panic even if you have plenty of time left. Work on pacing yourself so you can build confidence against the time constraints of the exam. Pacing is a difficult skill to master, especially in a high-pressure environment, so **practice is vital**.

Set time expectations for your pace based on how much time is available. For example, if a section has 60 questions and the time limit is 30 minutes, you know you have to average 30 seconds or less per question in order to answer them all. Although 30 seconds is the hard limit, set 25 seconds per question as your goal, so you reserve extra time to spend on harder questions. When you budget extra time for the harder questions, you no longer have any reason to stress when those questions take longer to answer.

Don't let this time expectation distract you from working through the test at a calm, steady pace, but keep it in mind so you don't spend too much time on any one question. Recognize that taking extra time on one question you don't understand may keep you from answering two that you do understand later in the test. If your time limit for a question is up and you're still not sure of the answer, mark it and move on, and come back to it later if the time and the test format allow. If the testing format doesn't allow you to return to earlier questions, just make an educated guess; then put it out of your mind and move on.

On the easier questions, be careful not to rush. It may seem wise to hurry through them so you have more time for the challenging ones, but it's not worth missing one if you know the concept and just didn't take the time to read the question fully. Work efficiently but make sure you understand the question and have looked at all of the answer choices, since more than one may seem right at first.

Even if you're paying attention to the time, you may find yourself a little behind at some point. You should speed up to get back on track, but do so wisely. Don't panic; just take a few seconds less on each question until you're caught up. Don't guess without thinking, but do look through the answer choices and eliminate any you know are wrong. If you can get down to two choices, it is often worthwhile to guess from those. Once you've chosen an answer, move on and don't dwell on any that you skipped or had to hurry through. If a question was taking too long, chances are it was one of the harder ones, so you weren't as likely to get it right anyway.

On the other hand, if you find yourself getting ahead of schedule, it may be beneficial to slow down a little. The more quickly you work, the more likely you are to make a careless mistake that will affect your score. You've budgeted time for each question, so don't be afraid to spend that time. Practice an efficient but careful pace to get the most out of the time you have.

Secret Key #5 – Have a Plan for Guessing

When you're taking the test, you may find yourself stuck on a question. Some of the answer choices seem better than others, but you don't see the one answer choice that is obviously correct. What do you do?

The scenario described above is very common, yet most test takers have not effectively prepared for it. Developing and practicing a plan for guessing may be one of the single most effective uses of your time as you get ready for the exam.

In developing your plan for guessing, there are three questions to address:

- When should you start the guessing process?
- How should you narrow down the choices?
- Which answer should you choose?

When to Start the Guessing Process

Unless your plan for guessing is to select C every time (which, despite its merits, is not what we recommend), you need to leave yourself enough time to apply your answer elimination strategies. Since you have a limited amount of time for each question, that means that if you're going to give yourself the best shot at guessing correctly, you have to decide quickly whether or not you will guess.

Of course, the best-case scenario is that you don't have to guess at all, so first, see if you can answer the question based on your knowledge of the subject and basic reasoning skills. Focus on the key words in the question and try to jog your memory of related topics. Give yourself a chance to bring the knowledge to mind, but once you realize that you don't have (or you can't access) the knowledge you need to answer the question, it's time to start the guessing process.

It's almost always better to start the guessing process too early than too late. It only takes a few seconds to remember something and answer the question from knowledge. Carefully eliminating wrong answer choices takes longer. Plus, going through the process of eliminating answer choices can actually help jog your memory.

Summary: Start the guessing process as soon as you decide that you can't answer the question based on your knowledge.

How to Narrow Down the Choices

The next chapter in this book (**Test-Taking Strategies**) includes a wide range of strategies for how to approach questions and how to look for answer choices to eliminate. You will definitely want to read those carefully, practice them, and figure out which ones work best for you. Here though, we're going to address a mindset rather than a particular strategy.

Your odds of guessing an answer correctly depend on how many options you are choosing from.

Number of options left	5	4	3	2	1
Odds of guessing correctly	20%	25%	33%	50%	100%

You can see from this chart just how valuable it is to be able to eliminate incorrect answers and make an educated guess, but there are two things that many test takers do that cause them to miss out on the benefits of guessing:

- Accidentally eliminating the correct answer
- Selecting an answer based on an impression

We'll look at the first one here, and the second one in the next section.

To avoid accidentally eliminating the correct answer, we recommend a thought exercise called **the $5 challenge**. In this challenge, you only eliminate an answer choice from contention if you are willing to bet $5 on it being wrong. Why $5? Five dollars is a small but not insignificant amount of money. It's an amount you could afford to lose but wouldn't want to throw away. And while losing $5 once might not hurt too much, doing it twenty times will set you back $100. In the same way, each small decision you make—eliminating a choice here, guessing on a question there—won't by itself impact your score very much, but when you put them all together, they can make a big difference. By holding each answer choice elimination decision to a higher standard, you can reduce the risk of accidentally eliminating the correct answer.

The $5 challenge can also be applied in a positive sense: If you are willing to bet $5 that an answer choice *is* correct, go ahead and mark it as correct.

Summary: Only eliminate an answer choice if you are willing to bet $5 that it is wrong.

Which Answer to Choose

You're taking the test. You've run into a hard question and decided you'll have to guess. You've eliminated all the answer choices you're willing to bet $5 on. Now you have to pick an answer. Why do we even need to talk about this? Why can't you just pick whichever one you feel like when the time comes?

The answer to these questions is that if you don't come into the test with a plan, you'll rely on your impression to select an answer choice, and if you do that, you risk falling into a trap. The test writers know that everyone who takes their test will be guessing on some of the questions, so they intentionally write wrong answer choices to seem plausible. You still have to pick an answer though, and if the wrong answer choices are designed to look right, how can you ever be sure that you're not falling for their trap? The best solution we've found to this dilemma is to take the decision out of your hands entirely. Here is the process we recommend:

Once you've eliminated any choices that you are confident (willing to bet $5) are wrong, select the first remaining choice as your answer.

Whether you choose to select the first remaining choice, the second, or the last, the important thing is that you use some preselected standard. Using this approach guarantees that you will not be enticed into selecting an answer choice that looks right, because you are not basing your decision on how the answer choices look.

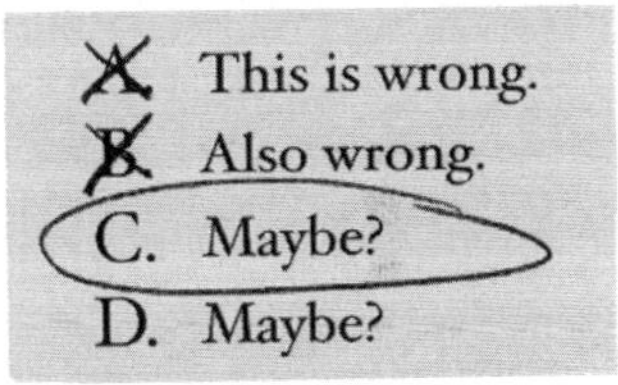

This is not meant to make you question your knowledge. Instead, it is to help you recognize the difference between your knowledge and your impressions. There's a huge difference between thinking an answer is right because of what you know, and thinking an answer is right because it looks or sounds like it should be right.

Summary: To ensure that your selection is appropriately random, make a predetermined selection from among all answer choices you have not eliminated.

Test-Taking Strategies

This section contains a list of test-taking strategies that you may find helpful as you work through the test. By taking what you know and applying logical thought, you can maximize your chances of answering any question correctly!

It is very important to realize that every question is different and every person is different: no single strategy will work on every question, and no single strategy will work for every person. That's why we've included all of them here, so you can try them out and determine which ones work best for different types of questions and which ones work best for you.

Question Strategies

✓ Read Carefully

Read the question and the answer choices carefully. Don't miss the question because you misread the terms. You have plenty of time to read each question thoroughly and make sure you understand what is being asked. Yet a happy medium must be attained, so don't waste too much time. You must read carefully and efficiently.

✓ Contextual Clues

Look for contextual clues. If the question includes a word you are not familiar with, look at the immediate context for some indication of what the word might mean. Contextual clues can often give you all the information you need to decipher the meaning of an unfamiliar word. Even if you can't determine the meaning, you may be able to narrow down the possibilities enough to make a solid guess at the answer to the question.

✓ Prefixes

If you're having trouble with a word in the question or answer choices, try dissecting it. Take advantage of every clue that the word might include. Prefixes can be a huge help. Usually, they allow you to determine a basic meaning. *Pre-* means before, *post-* means after, *pro-* is positive, *de-* is negative. From prefixes, you can get an idea of the general meaning of the word and try to put it into context.

✓ Hedge Words

Watch out for critical hedge words, such as *likely, may, can, often, almost, mostly, usually, generally, rarely,* and *sometimes.* Question writers insert these hedge phrases to cover every possibility. Often an answer choice will be wrong simply because it leaves no room for exception. Be on guard for answer choices that have definitive words such as *exactly* and *always.*

✓ Switchback Words

Stay alert for *switchbacks.* These are the words and phrases frequently used to alert you to shifts in thought. The most common switchback words are *but, although,* and *however.* Others include *nevertheless, on the other hand, even though, while, in spite of, despite,* and *regardless of.* Switchback words are important to catch because they can change the direction of the question or an answer choice.

⊘ FACE VALUE

When in doubt, use common sense. Accept the situation in the problem at face value. Don't read too much into it. These problems will not require you to make wild assumptions. If you have to go beyond creativity and warp time or space in order to have an answer choice fit the question, then you should move on and consider the other answer choices. These are normal problems rooted in reality. The applicable relationship or explanation may not be readily apparent, but it is there for you to figure out. Use your common sense to interpret anything that isn't clear.

Answer Choice Strategies

⊘ ANSWER SELECTION

The most thorough way to pick an answer choice is to identify and eliminate wrong answers until only one is left, then confirm it is the correct answer. Sometimes an answer choice may immediately seem right, but be careful. The test writers will usually put more than one reasonable answer choice on each question, so take a second to read all of them and make sure that the other choices are not equally obvious. As long as you have time left, it is better to read every answer choice than to pick the first one that looks right without checking the others.

⊘ ANSWER CHOICE FAMILIES

An answer choice family consists of two (in rare cases, three) answer choices that are very similar in construction and cannot all be true at the same time. If you see two answer choices that are direct opposites or parallels, one of them is usually the correct answer. For instance, if one answer choice says that quantity x increases and another either says that quantity x decreases (opposite) or says that quantity y increases (parallel), then those answer choices would fall into the same family. An answer choice that doesn't match the construction of the answer choice family is more likely to be incorrect. Most questions will not have answer choice families, but when they do appear, you should be prepared to recognize them.

⊘ ELIMINATE ANSWERS

Eliminate answer choices as soon as you realize they are wrong, but make sure you consider all possibilities. If you are eliminating answer choices and realize that the last one you are left with is also wrong, don't panic. Start over and consider each choice again. There may be something you missed the first time that you will realize on the second pass.

⊘ AVOID FACT TRAPS

Don't be distracted by an answer choice that is factually true but doesn't answer the question. You are looking for the choice that answers the question. Stay focused on what the question is asking for so you don't accidentally pick an answer that is true but incorrect. Always go back to the question and make sure the answer choice you've selected actually answers the question and is not merely a true statement.

⊘ EXTREME STATEMENTS

In general, you should avoid answers that put forth extreme actions as standard practice or proclaim controversial ideas as established fact. An answer choice that states the "process should be used in certain situations, if…" is much more likely to be correct than one that states the "process should be discontinued completely." The first is a calm rational statement and doesn't even make a definitive, uncompromising stance, using a hedge word *if* to provide wiggle room, whereas the second choice is far more extreme.

☑ BENCHMARK

As you read through the answer choices and you come across one that seems to answer the question well, mentally select that answer choice. This is not your final answer, but it's the one that will help you evaluate the other answer choices. The one that you selected is your benchmark or standard for judging each of the other answer choices. Every other answer choice must be compared to your benchmark. That choice is correct until proven otherwise by another answer choice beating it. If you find a better answer, then that one becomes your new benchmark. Once you've decided that no other choice answers the question as well as your benchmark, you have your final answer.

☑ PREDICT THE ANSWER

Before you even start looking at the answer choices, it is often best to try to predict the answer. When you come up with the answer on your own, it is easier to avoid distractions and traps because you will know exactly what to look for. The right answer choice is unlikely to be word-for-word what you came up with, but it should be a close match. Even if you are confident that you have the right answer, you should still take the time to read each option before moving on.

General Strategies

☑ TOUGH QUESTIONS

If you are stumped on a problem or it appears too hard or too difficult, don't waste time. Move on! Remember though, if you can quickly check for obviously incorrect answer choices, your chances of guessing correctly are greatly improved. Before you completely give up, at least try to knock out a couple of possible answers. Eliminate what you can and then guess at the remaining answer choices before moving on.

☑ CHECK YOUR WORK

Since you will probably not know every term listed and the answer to every question, it is important that you get credit for the ones that you do know. Don't miss any questions through careless mistakes. If at all possible, try to take a second to look back over your answer selection and make sure you've selected the correct answer choice and haven't made a costly careless mistake (such as marking an answer choice that you didn't mean to mark). This quick double check should more than pay for itself in caught mistakes for the time it costs.

☑ PACE YOURSELF

It's easy to be overwhelmed when you're looking at a page full of questions; your mind is confused and full of random thoughts, and the clock is ticking down faster than you would like. Calm down and maintain the pace that you have set for yourself. Especially as you get down to the last few minutes of the test, don't let the small numbers on the clock make you panic. As long as you are on track by monitoring your pace, you are guaranteed to have time for each question.

☑ DON'T RUSH

It is very easy to make errors when you are in a hurry. Maintaining a fast pace in answering questions is pointless if it makes you miss questions that you would have gotten right otherwise. Test writers like to include distracting information and wrong answers that seem right. Taking a little extra time to avoid careless mistakes can make all the difference in your test score. Find a pace that allows you to be confident in the answers that you select.

⊘ Keep Moving

Panicking will not help you pass the test, so do your best to stay calm and keep moving. Taking deep breaths and going through the answer elimination steps you practiced can help to break through a stress barrier and keep your pace.

Final Notes

The combination of a solid foundation of content knowledge and the confidence that comes from practicing your plan for applying that knowledge is the key to maximizing your performance on test day. As your foundation of content knowledge is built up and strengthened, you'll find that the strategies included in this chapter become more and more effective in helping you quickly sift through the distractions and traps of the test to isolate the correct answer.

Now that you're preparing to move forward into the test content chapters of this book, be sure to keep your goal in mind. As you read, think about how you will be able to apply this information on the test. If you've already seen sample questions for the test and you have an idea of the question format and style, try to come up with questions of your own that you can answer based on what you're reading. This will give you valuable practice applying your knowledge in the same ways you can expect to on test day.

Good luck and good studying!

Six Sigma Fundamentals

PRODUCT DFSS IMPLEMENTATION

A design for Six Sigma project can take many forms, but a general path for product DFSS implementation exists. The first step is a meeting between the Six Sigma black belt and champion. At this meeting, the two experts consider the business from a long distance, what is known in Six Sigma as the satellite view. They then will isolate some important metrics and relate them to business needs, with the intention of finding areas in which the existing range of products could be expanded or enhanced. The black belt and champion might brainstorm a list of similar products, so the development processes used in the past can be evaluated. The champion and black belt will generate a set of slightly more close-up metrics, from what is known as the 30,000-foot level. The intention of these measurements is to shift the focus from the developed products to the process of product development. Finally, the champion and black belt will draft a project charter.

After drafting a project charter, the Six Sigma black belt and champion of a typical product DFSS project will devise a strategy for meeting the customer's requirements. Then these experts will create a team of key stakeholders. At this point, the black belt, champion, and stakeholders will have their initial meeting. One of the key items on the meeting's agenda will be the resolution of any issues that could interfere with regular status reporting or the structure of the project. The team will cooperate to produce problem and goal statements. They also will create a SIPOC diagram and a gap analysis of the product development process to customer needs. Using a high-level process map, the team will take a closer look at the development process. The black belt is in charge of ensuring that the selected 30,000-foot metrics are aligned with the satellite-level metrics.

After leading the initial project team meeting, the black belt in charge of a product DFSS project will meet with the finance department. The purpose of this meeting will be to establish the possible business impact of the fledgling project. The finance department should help the black belt outline the financial issues related to the project, and the two parties should agree on appropriate financial metrics. The black belt should make sure that the financial analysis includes an indication of how the project could reduce costs in the long run. In many projects, the analyses of designed experiment results are useful for predicting the financial benefits of a possible solution. The team then can make a general plan of the project, and if it will be useful, compose a Gantt chart.

After creating a Gantt chart for the new product DFSS project, the Six Sigma team will collect some data from similar projects. In particular, the team will determine the most useful metrics from past product development projects. These metrics should be displayed in time-series format, so the chronological order of previous products is apparent. At this point, the Six Sigma team will create control or run charts of key process output variables (KPOVs) from the 30,000-foot level. Some of the most important KPOVs are return on investment from the product and development cycle time. These control charts should be able to isolate places in which the product development process was affected significantly by special causes of variation. If the products all have responses that lie within the control limits, then any variation is the result of noise during the product development process. All of this work will be based on the business' data records, so an operational archiving program is important.

In a Six Sigma project focused on processes, metrics typically are based on specifications, which in turn are based on customer preferences. This arrangement usually is inappropriate for a product DFSS project, however. For product DFSS, metrics more often are based on long-term capability and performance. In particular, many projects use frequency of occurrence as a primary metric. For instance, a project might determine how often a product development team completes a cycle within a given amount of time (e.g., "70% of development projects are completed in between 6.2 and 7.5 months"). As with all Six Sigma metrics, expressing in monetary terms is important. Once appropriate metrics have been identified, previous products should be evaluated to identify recurrent nonconformance issues. These issues can be plotted on a Pareto chart. These Pareto charts often reveal that what appeared secondary or insignificant problems actually are responsible for severe delays or deviations.

After nonconformance issues are plotted on a Pareto chart, the typical product DFSS project will continue with the creation of a detailed process flowchart or map. This chart or map must be created with sufficient detail to indicate other possible courses of action. The black belt and team also should pay attention to the manner of collecting information about customers as well as the impact of voice-of-the-customer inputs on product development. There should also be some mechanism for identifying issues related to cycle time. Many product DFSS teams find that lean tools such as time-value diagrams and value stream analysis are good for this purpose. In any case, the next step for the project team will be to create a cause-and-effect diagram of the key process output variables. The selection of entries for this diagram will be based on the process flowchart and Pareto chart.

Using their new cause-and-effect diagram, the Six Sigma team then will identify the strength of the relationships between process input and output variables on a cause-and-effect matrix. If the matrix is effective, it will indicate the most important input variables. These input variables then can be ranked on a Pareto chart, thus suggesting the key process input variables. The next step is the creation of a detailed failure modes and effects analysis in which the inputs are the steps in product development. In some cases, a systems point of view is more appropriate than other points of view. If this approach is used, the input items will be the most significant values in the cause-and-effect matrix. At this point, it assessing the current control plans is appropriate. The failure modes and effects analysis should consider whether the current battery of development tests and measurement systems are risky. Performing a measurement systems analysis might be necessary. This is also a good time to consider applying the theory of inventive problem-solving, designed experiments, DOE collective response capability assessment, or simplified quality function deployment.

After creating and applying the failure modes and effects analysis, the product DFSS team often will gather data from earlier development projects and examine closely the relationships between key process input and output variables. If this task is successful, identifying sources of process variability will be possible. These sources then can be represented visually on multi-vari charts, marginal plots, box plots, and other media. The statistical significance of the relationships between key process input and output variables can be assessed with hypothesis tests. If a great deal of information from previous product development cycles exists, the origins of output variability may be suggested by variance components analysis. Moreover, when significant historical data exists it may be possible to perform analyses of variance, analyses of means, correlation studies, and regressions, all of which may illuminate the influence of KPIVs on KPOVs.

After completing a battery of studies on the statistical significance of KPIVs on KPOVs, the product DFSS team will assess the manufacturing, supplier, and design elements of the development process with response surface analysis, pass/fail functional testing, and designed experiments. Obviously, assessments of the manufacturing elements are necessary only when noticeable variation has occurred in key process output variables during the manufacturing process. For instance, when significant variation in the quality of raw material exists, it might be appropriate to design experiments that identify KPIV adjustments to make the process more resistant to noise. When the current set of reliability tests have done a poor job of predicting product failure rates, applied DOE may prove an effective replacement or addition. Many product DFSS teams conclude that DOE should be implemented as a control methodology in the development process. In any case, designed experiments and other methods can indicate the best operating windows for KPIVs with regard to manufacturing.

After using DOEs and other methods to identify the KPIV operating windows with the best impact on manufacturing, the product DFSS team will update the control plan. During this task, a product development control plan may include pass/fail functional testing methodologies, fractional factorial DOE experiments, and reliability assessments, which all can be important. The control plan also should indicate how the development department (and other departments) will intervene whenever problems occur. Finally, the product DFSS team will verify the process improvements, stability, performance, and capability going forward. The team will gather to create a final project report summarizing the benefits of the project, including the financial benefits. This project report should be disseminated throughout the organization.

Process DFSS Implementation

A typical process DFSS implementation begins with the black belt and champion analyzing extremely long-distance metrics, known in Six Sigma as satellite-level metrics. When this analysis suggests a business need to create a new process, then a process DFSS project is warranted. The next step for the black belt and champion is to compose a project charter. This document should include a general plan for project implementation. Around this time, the black belt should indicate the way in which the financial benefits of the program will be calculated. Then, stakeholders are identified and a team is formed. The next step in the Six Sigma project will be to define its customers, whether internal or external. At an initial team meeting, the black belt, champion, and proposed team members will consider a problem statement, goal statement, and a gap analysis of the process to customer needs. The team also will analyze some 30,000-foot-level metrics, and make sure that these metrics align with the metrics obtained from the satellite level.

After aligning the 30,000-foot-level metrics with the satellite-level metrics, the process DFSS project team will define the key project output variables to be tracked during the project. Identifying the types of defects to be tracked and determining a method for calculating overall throughput time is important. Next, the black belt and team will gather to collect and record the voice-of-customer needs and desires with respect to the process, which is done with quality function deployment and other tools related to voice of the customer. In addition, identifying the desired values for 30,000-foot-level metrics is necessary. After doing this, the Six Sigma team and black belt will benchmark similar processes and create a flowchart that represents the process needs. The next step will be to consider applying lean tools such as the logic flow map, time-value diagram, and spaghetti chart. If necessary, the process can be tweaked at this point.

After applying lean tools and making any necessary adjustments to the process plan, the process DFSS project team will create a project management plan for actually creating the process. At this point the team should discuss the implications of modeling the process with a process modeling computer program. The next step will be to conduct a process failure modes and effects analysis. This analysis will indicate the appropriate changes for the process. Next, the black belt and team will create a list of all the variables likely to be key process input variables, or KPIVs. The process DFSS project team will then perform a DOE (design of experiments) that simulates the process. In addition, the process DFSS project team may want to apply pass/fail functional tests. If the tests indicate extreme values for key process input variables, then this information should be taken into consideration during the design of experiments.

The typical process DFSS project team first will conduct DOE and then will compose a DOE collective response capability assessment (DCRCA). As part of the DCRCA, the team will create a probability plot of the DOE responses and then compare them to the customer requirements relative to the process. The next step will be to use basic procedures for analyzing DOE should the desired percentage points from a probability plot fall outside the conformance levels. Next, the team must adjust the process design, which is done with the knowledge obtained from DOE. If done properly, the subsequent DOE should deliver the desired results. Next, the process DFSS project team will create a control plan related to the key process input variables found to be statistically significant. The subsequent step is to finish the plan for monitoring key process output variables from the 30,000-foot level.

After finishing the plan for tracking key process output variables from the 30,000-foot level, the process DFSS project team typically will gather and organize the key process output variables as a function of key process input variables. This step is done in case closer investigation of causes is required in the future. Next, the team will update and abide by the project management plan for process creation. The process DFSS team then will run a pilot for the finished process. During this pilot run, key process output variables must be tracked at the 30,000-foot level. Next, the team must determine whether the desired levels of the process have been met by the capability and performance. When desired levels are not met, a DMAIC strategy may be implemented for process improvement. Once the process has been brought to the desired level, the results of the project should be documented and passed around the organization. If the results of this project can be applied to other areas of the business, this should be the focus of future projects.

Six Sigma

Six Sigma is a program for improving business processes. The name is derived from the Greek letter sigma, or σ, used in statistics to indicate the standard deviation for a particular set of data. The standard deviation suggests the amount of variation between the members of the data set. Statisticians describe variation in terms of units of standard deviation, or sigma units, in order to provide a more accurate picture. Imagine a process that can be represented graphically as a bell curve. The centerline of the process is a time of 25 minutes, meaning that this is the average time required to complete the process. If the standard deviation is 30 seconds, then six standard deviations, or 6σ, would be either 22 minutes or 28 minutes. The general intention of Six Sigma is to improve all business processes such that six standard deviations will fit between the mean and both the upper and lower acceptable limits.

Application of Six Sigma Tools in Manufacturing Process

A Six Sigma project related to a manufacturing process can take any number of forms, but all such projects feature a general trajectory. A typical manufacturing project will begin with a meeting between the black belt and champion. These two employees will take an extremely long-distance look at the organization, sometimes called a "satellite view," and identify a pressing business need. This need should be considered in terms of customer requirements. The black belt and champion will establish the project scope and draft the project charter. Next, they will identify the key process output variables (KPOVs) to be measured. The next step in the typical manufacturing project will be to identify the key stakeholders and conduct an initial meeting. The fledgling team will consider any issues likely to interfere with status reporting or the project schedule. At the initial meeting, the team, the champion, and the process owner will consider the problem and goal statements. They also will create a gap analysis of the process to customer needs and a SIPOC diagram.

After conducting the initial meeting, the black belt in charge of a manufacturing project will meet with the finance department to determine the monetary impact of the proposed project. The black belt and the finance department will agree on appropriate financial metrics for the project. They will also calculate the cost of poor quality (COPQ) and the cost of doing nothing different (CODND). After finishing with the finance department, the black belt will identify the customer data required for the project. The black belt also will define the secondary metrics such as rolled throughput yield. The black belt and team then will create a general project plan and perhaps create a Gantt chart for guidance. The black belt and team then will compose control or run charts for the key process output variables (KPOVs). These charts should be taken from a considerable distance, known in Six Sigma as the 30,000-foot level. A set of charts from this distance will obviate problems later in the project.

After drafting run and control charts from the 30,000-foot level, the black belt heading up a typical manufacturing project will lead the team in the identification of long-term process capability and performance metrics for the key process output variables. These metrics will be based on the aforementioned control charts. All of the relevant nonconformance issues can be organized on a Pareto chart. At this point, revising the costs of poor quality and doing nothing different may be necessary. The next step in the project will be to compose a process map or flowchart with enough specificity to indicate possible problems. Using lean manufacturing tools might be useful at this point. The next move will be to generate a cause-and-effect diagram that suggests the variables related to process output. The entries for this diagram may be based on the process flowchart and the Pareto chart of nonconformance issues.

After creating a cause-and-effect diagram of all the process input variables, a Six Sigma manufacturing project team will make a cause-and-effect matrix indicating the strength of the relationships between the process input and output variables. Next, the team will take a step back and perform a measurement systems analysis. This analysis tests the integrity of the collected data. Another approach is to assess the repeatability and reproducibility of the measurements with a variance components analysis. This latter analysis also will assess the variations between different machines. The team will then place the input variables from the cause-and-effect matrix on a Pareto chart. The Pareto chart should identify the possible key process input variables (KPIVs). Next, the team will prepare a targeted failure modes and effects analysis. In most cases, the FMEA should be from a systems perspective, and the input items should be the most important sources of variation identified by the cause-and-effect matrix. The team then will need to assess the current control plans and implement the first set of process improvements.

After implementing the first set of process improvements, the typical manufacturing project team will create a plan for data collection. They will begin to gather data related to the relationships between key process input and output variables (i.e., KPIVs and KPOVs). The next step is to represent graphically the sources of process variation. Some of the tools useful for this representation are multi-vari charts, box plots, and marginal plots. The black belt and team then can use hypothesis tests to determine the statistical significance of the relationships. It may be useful at this point to perform a variance components analysis related to the sources of output variability. In some instances, there will be variation based on the day of the week or the particular machine. The relationship between KPIVs and KPOVs is further explored though statistical studies such as regression and correlation analysis, analysis of variance, and analysis of means. After all of this analysis, the next batch of process improvements may be implemented.

After implementing the second batch of process improvements, the typical Six Sigma manufacturing project team will decide whether to conduct designed experiments and response surface analyses. In many projects, the experiments will be organized with the intention of making the process more robust with respect to raw material variability and other noise factors. The Six Sigma team then will use the results of designed experiments to identify the best operating windows for key process input variables (KPIVs). This task should suggest some process improvements, which then may be implemented. The team will then error-proof the key process inputs as much as possible and update the control plan. The typical manufacturing project team then will apply control charts from a moderate distance, known in Six Sigma as the fifty-foot level. These control charts are useful for identifying special causes of variation in key process input variables.

After the Six Sigma team has composed control charts from the fifty-foot level, they will set about confirming the process improvements, as well as the process stability, capability, and performance. All of these values should be obtained through demonstration runs. The team then will create a final project report outlining all of the benefits, especially the financial benefits, of the project. This project report should be made available to every member of the organization. The improvements made by the project might apply to other areas of the organization. After meeting with the process owner, the Six Sigma black belt and team gradually can divest themselves of responsibility for the process. However, the champion and black belt should monitor process performance at three and six months after completion of the project.

Application of Six Sigma Tools in Service or Transactional Process

While no single way describes the application of Six Sigma tools to service or transactional processes, several rough guidelines exist. First, a Six Sigma black belt and champion would take a distanced look at the organization to identify business needs. Finding critical customer needs that can be measured from a distance is important. The black belt and champion then would define the scope of a Six Sigma project and draft a project charter. The next step would be to identify the key process output variables (KPOVs) for the project metrics. At this point, the black belt and champion would identify a team of key stakeholders and conduct an initial meeting. They would discuss the problem statement, gap analysis, goal statement, and SIPOC diagram. The black belt then would meet with the finance department to discuss the business impact of the project and the financial metrics that should be used. They also would calculate the cost of poor quality (COPQ) and the cost of doing nothing different (CODND).

While the Six Sigma black belt is meeting with the finance department, the champion and the rest of the team can be determining the customer information required for the project. This group also could be identifying potentially useful secondary metrics. At this point many teams will find it a good idea to create a Gantt chart. Next, the black belt and team would begin compiling project metrics in a time series format with infrequent subgrouping or sampling. The team should create control charts or run charts for the key process output variables. In other Six Sigma projects, this time would prent the opportunity to concentrate on specifications. However, in service or transactional processes, considering long-term capability and performance metrics in either frequency of occurrence units or percentage beyond desired value is appropriate. These measures should be placed in financial terms and used as base-line performance. All of the nonconformance issues associated with this process should be placed on a Pareto chart.

After making a Pareto chart of all the nonconformance issues related to the process, the Six Sigma black belt and the rest of the team could create a detailed flowchart or process map and study it for possible areas of improvement. At this time, the team could implement some lean methodologies. The black belt and team then would draw up a cause-and-effect diagram to look for variables that affect outputs. This diagram can be assembled with the help of the process flowchart and Pareto chart. Next, the black belt and team could create a cause-and-effect matrix in which the relationships between input variables and key process output variables are considered. The data collected can be assessed with a measurement systems analysis, especially in situations where nonconformance issues may be classified incorrectly.

In a typical Six Sigma project related to a service or transactional process, the measurement systems analysis would be followed by the application of a Pareto chart to the cause-and-effect matrix. Specifically, the black belt and the rest of the Six Sigma team will use the Pareto chart to indicate the relative importance of the input variables identified by the matrix. The resulting Pareto chart will suggest the key process input variables (KPIVs). The next step will be to prepare a failure modes and effects analysis and evaluate the current control plans. The team then will make a plan for data collection and begin implementing some initial changes to the process. The collected data must bear on the suspected relationships between KPIVs and KPOVs. The team then will attempt to depict the sources of variability in forms such as box plots, marginal plots, and multi-vari charts. The statistical significance of relationships between KPIVs and KPOVs may be evaluated with hypothesis tests.

After using hypothesis tests to find the statistical significance of the relationships between KPIVs and KPOVs, the black belt leading a project based on a service or transactional process will decide whether to investigate output variability by performing variance components analysis. For example, the black belt might be interested in the differences between departments or times of day. Next, the black belt would oversee statistical studies related to the impact of KPIVs on KPOVs. These may include correlation and regression studies, analyses of variance, and analyses of means. The team then will implement another set of process improvements. At this point, the team will decide whether to perform designed experiments to test the possible impact of process change ideas. In many cases, these experiments will provide insight into the relationships between change ideas and noise factors.

After performing any advisable designed experiments, the black belt in charge of a service or transactional project will calculate the best operating windows of the key process input variables (KPIVs). The control plan will need to be updated at this point, and control charts should be implemented to identify special-cause variation related to KPIVs. The final tasks for the black belt and team are to confirm the process improvements, stability, and performance metrics. This confirmation should be done through targeted demonstration runs. At this point, the black belt should bring the Six Sigma champion and process owners back into the project. The entire Six Sigma team will create a final project report and indicate the financial benefits of the project. This complete report should be disseminated or at least made available throughout the organization. If possible, the results of the project should be applied to problems elsewhere in the business. Responsibility for the process should be returned to the process owner. Performance should be monitored at three and six months after the end of the project.

Six Sigma Champions

Qualifications

In Six Sigma, champions are managers who oversee projects and ensure the projects align with the broader strategic goals of the organization. Most companies initiate their Six Sigma program by selecting and training a set of champions. These champions in turn select the first batch of black belts. Some basic personal and professional requirements apply to champions. A champion, first, should be energized by Six Sigma. The champions who introduce Six Sigma to the rest of the company's employees must be enthusiastic capable of transferring that enthusiasm. As a result, a Six Sigma champion must have charisma. He or she must possess respect within the organization. In addition, a champion should have the technical skills to supervise Six Sigma implementation. A champion should be able to align Six Sigma projects with customer desires. Champions should know how to represent Six Sigma projects in objective terms.

Training

Champions typically are the first members of an organization to be trained in Six Sigma, so it is especially important for their training to be effective. In most cases, the first step in champion training is a basic class lasting two or three days. The focus of this introductory course is the role of champions in building a Six Sigma program. Champion training always should include workshops in which participants are given the chance to practice some of the techniques they are learning. Part of the training should focus on the selection of black belt and green belt candidates. Another part should focus on the selection of appropriate projects. The majority of the training session, however, should be a crash course in the basics of Six Sigma. Aspiring champions should learn about the merits of the program, as well as about its differences with other systems of quality management and continuous improvement.

Lean

Lean is a comprehensive system for decreasing waste and increasing cycle times and quality. The tools of lean (e.g. 5S, velocity, spaghetti diagrams, level loading, and process cycle efficiency), are used in every phase of DMAIC. Many of the ideas of lean date back to Henry Ford, but the credit for assembling and updating the system goes to Taiichi Ohno, an employee of Toyota in the 1970s. In Japan, the philosophy is called *muda*. The general strategy of lean is to identify activities that add value and activities that do not add value. As much as possible, lean businesses try to eliminate activities that do not add value. These judgments always are made from the perspective of the consumer. Lean methodology is very similar in this respect to Six Sigma.

Transparency, Velocity, and Value

The lean philosophy emphasizes three areas: transparency, velocity, and value. Transparency is easy access to useful information. A business has achieved transparency when processes can be observed and measured. Errors should be noticed immediately and rectified. Velocity, meanwhile, is the speed with which processes are completed. The ultimate measure of velocity is the interval between a customer's order and the delivery of the good or service. In lean methodology, velocity is sometimes called flow. The goal of lean is to reduce process lead times and enable the business to respond quickly and agilely to customer requests. Finally, value is the set of qualities or characteristics for which a customer is willing to pay. The goal of lean is to increase value and diminish waste. Value always is assessed from the perspective of the customer.

Inventory

In lean methodology, inventory and work-in-progress are considered drags on progress rather than assets. A lean business will try to keep very little inventory on hand and instead will strive to respond quickly to customer orders without relying on the storage of works-in-progress. A general habit involves finishing work in progress before handling new orders, which slows down production. Lean emphasizes other strategies for improving velocity. For instance, business can find ways to increase the number of completions per hour or eliminate redundant or unnecessary process steps. A business could improve velocity by decreasing errors or waiting time. A business also could improve velocity by decreasing the necessity of moving resources or personnel. When velocity is increased through these strategies, value tends to increase as well.

Error-Proofing Strategies

Error-proofing, often referred to with the Japanese term *poka-yoke*, is a system for preventing defects in production processes. The poka-yoke philosophy asserts that preventing errors is better than detecting them, so processes should be analyzed rigorously and improved so mistakes occur less often. One form of error-proofing is auto-correction systems, which reflexively adjust to changing external conditions. Another form of error-proofing is an automatic shutdown, which stops a machine or process if conditions for an error exist. A final form of error-proofing is the warning signal, which of course depends on the presence of a human operator. Nevertheless, a warning signal can be an effective alert that an error is about to occur. Error-proofing strategies can be expensive to implement and may slow processes at first, but in the long run these strategies will save money and time that would have been wasted on mistakes.

Value Stream Mapping

Value stream mapping is a communication tool for Six Sigma professionals. It depicts the flow of materials and information through an organization. Most value stream maps have two versions: a current state and a future state. The future state map depicts the process after planned improvements have been made. Ideally, the future state version of the value stream map will be less complicated than the current state. Value stream maps are effective when they identify waste and redundancy in processes. Each activity in a process should be represented with a shape on the map. Furthermore, each activity should be accompanied by the following information: cycle time, down time, in-process inventory, path of information, and path of materials. After a current state value map has been produced, it should be examined for steps that do not add value. These steps should be eliminated or minimized.

Seven Classic Wastes

The Japanese waste-reduction system referred to as *muda* considers seven classic wastes: transportation, inventory, motion, waiting (work-in-progress), over-processing, over-production, and defects. Transportation is a source of waste because moving products and materials risks damaging or losing them. Transportation is not considered a value-added activity. Inventory is considered a waste because it does not contribute to income. Motion is distinct from transportation in that it refers only to the movement of the product during the production process. Waiting, also known as work-in-progress, is defined as the time when goods are neither being processed nor in transport. Over-processing occurs when more work than is necessary is performed on a product. One common form of over-processing is the use of tools or equipment much nicer than the process requires. Over-production occurs when the amount or number of goods produced exceeds the demands of customers. Defects are errors that necessitate reworking or rescheduling.

Kanban

Kanban, a Japanese term roughly translated as "billboard," is a scheduling system that helps businesses make production decisions. The kanban system is based on the operations of a supermarket. The developers of the system noticed that in a supermarket, customers get what they want and the store stocks only what it knows will sell. The developers of kanban decided to treat manufacturing like a supermarket, where each process acts like a customer, selecting the items it needs from inventory and previous processes. One of the chief insights of kanban is that products should not be pushed along from task to task, but instead pulled by the void created by task completion. In other words, when a task is completed, the operator should look to the previous steps for more work. The result of this approach is that inventories are smaller and work is more continuous. In the kanban system, cards are used to indicate demand in subsequent steps of the production path.

Kanban Cards and Three-Bin-System

Kanban cards indicate when a work station is ready to receive more materials. The card is displayed when the operator needs more products, parts, or inventory to continue his or her work. These cards are displayed in all sorts of ways: in some companies, they are affixed to posts next to each work station, while in other companies they are dropped into empty containers to encourage refilling. Electronic kanban systems now eschew physical cards in favor of computerized alerts. One of the most common forms of kanban is the three-bin system, with containers on the factory floor, in the factory store, and in the supplier's store. Each of these bins will contain a kanban card indicating the product details and other important information. If the factory floor bin is empty, it is returned to the factory store along with the kanban cards. A full bin is then sent from the factory store to the factory floor. This bin includes a kanban card. At this point, the factory store returns the empty bin and kanban card to the supplier's store. Finally, the supplier returns a full bin to the factory store accompanied by a kanban card.

Key Performance Indicators

Key performance indicators (KPIs) are metrics monitored by the entire organization to ensure that a strategic plan is being followed. Key performance indicators show the degree to which the business has achieved its goals, or at least the progress made. They indicate when continuous improvement programs are successful or need to be adjusted. Also, key performance indicators provide context for regular meetings between management and employees. KPIs make it possible for every member of the business to understand whether performance is acceptable. A key performance indicator should be tied directly to strategic goals. Of course, strategic goals must be written such that they can be objectively assessed. KPIs should relate to customer desires, whether those customers are internal and external. KPIs should be somewhat easy to obtain. Finally, they should be able to identify waste and inefficiency.

Product Performance and Performance on Quality Improvement

Certain key performance indicators commonly identify when a business is adhering to its strategic plan. Product performance metrics supply data about the features and functions of products. This data should be objective and should include all of the product's features and functions. Performance on quality improvement is a metric used by businesses that run a number of different strategic plans at the same time. The performance on quality improvement metric indicates the number of projects completed and ongoing; the financial results; and the employees involved in each of these efforts. The financial results of quality improvement projects include the amounts gained, the amounts invested, and the return on investment. The performance on quality improvement metric enables a business to compare projects that may be quite different.

Competitive Quality and Cost of Poor Quality

Competitive quality metrics focus on the aspects of performance that influence product sales. These aspects could include the speed of transactions, the degree to which customers are pleased with service, and the accuracy of order fulfillment. In some industries, competitive quality metrics will indicate the extent to which the delivered product meets the expectations of the consumer. Some of this information must be obtained directly from customers, which means the business may need to solicit or pay for it. The cost of poor quality metric is the gap between current costs and the costs that would be incurred without any waste, error, or inefficiency. The cost of poor quality gives a business a target and a motivation for improvement efforts. Of course, the precise value of the cost of poor quality cannot be known. Most businesses develop programs for estimating the cost of poor quality in the most significant areas.

Performance of Business Processes and Product and Process Deficiencies

Performance of business processes metrics only recently have been refined to the point that they can be used as key performance indicators. In most organizations, business processes are so large and disparate that they are difficult to measure. Businesses should establish internal standards for cycle time, errors, and other relevant values. Another tricky KPI is product and process deficiency. These are represented in a manner similar to cost of poor quality. For instance, a business might determine the cost of poor quality for every hour of work or for every shipped product. These values contribute to the overall picture of the cost of poor quality, which itself can be difficult to calculate. Generating values for product and process deficiencies is important because these values can be compared between products and departments.

Business Performance Measures

Revenue Growth, Market Share, and Margin

Revenue growth indicates the change in sales figures over time. Essentially, revenue is the money that a business brings in through its operations. If revenue is growing, then the business should have more money to reinvest and make capital improvements. Of course, growth in revenue can be offset by growth in expenses. Market share, meanwhile, is the portion of a given market services by a business. Market share provides information about the level of competition in a market, but it does not necessarily indicate whether a business is serving the market efficiently. A business may believe that because it holds a large market share it does not need to continue working to serve its customers. Finally, margin is the amount of money a business needs to create in order to sustain operations. Obviously, businesses want to earn profits far in excess of the margin, but they also should consider whether profits are being reinvested effectively in order to create the conditions for long-term growth.

Cost of Quality, Net Present Value, Return on Investment

Cost of quality is a measure of the financial resources required to create a good product or service. Businesses isolate those costs that directly influence the quality of their work and focus on these costs in their reinvestment and capital improvement strategies. Although higher quality generally entails higher cost, continuous attention to the specific factors that influence quality can result in lower costs without the sacrifice of quality. Net present value is the difference between the current worth of cash inflows and the current worth of cash outflows. This measure is used in investment decisions. If the money expected in the future from an investment is greater than the money required at present, the investment is a good idea. Finally, return on investment is the money recouped after an initial outlay. Businesses keep track of ROI to determine whether capital improvements and investments have been wise.

Resolving Feuds Within Teams

Every Six Sigma team contains a range of personalities, some of which inevitably will come into conflict. In many cases, the members of a Six Sigma team will have worked on the same process or in the same department for a long time and will have long-standing disagreements. This behavior is extremely counterproductive to the goals of the team and must be rooted out as soon as detected. Various approaches exist in regard to conflict resolution, such as arbitration, counseling, and peer mediation. Usually these problems should be handled by someone outside the team, since any intervention by a team member could be seen as taking sides. If the conflicting team members are essential to the success of the project and their dispute appears irreconcilable, they should be separated as much as possible. The black belt also should monitor this situation closely and should have individual consultations with all parties concerned throughout the course of the project.

Reducing Unfocused Conversation and Digressions

One common problem in business meetings is inefficient conversational habits such as digressions or tangents. The black belt is responsible for ensuring that team communication remains focused and controlled. Every meeting should follow a strict agenda and should adhere to time constraints. Making a meeting open-ended is an invitation to time-wasting. In some cases, it is useful to set time limits for each item on the agenda. The black belt may want to designate some other team member as the time-keeper during meetings, since the black belt most likely will be busy with other matters. The time-keeper should have the authority to interrupt conversation and remind the team members of the agenda. However, sometimes unexpected issues will arise, and the black belt should be prepared to adjust the established time limits if fruitful conversation is occurring.

Avoiding Discounting Participation By Team Members

Every member of a Six Sigma team is selected because they have unique and necessary skills. For this reason, every team member should feel that his or her insights and ideas are valued. The black belt or project leader should avoid situations in which a team member feels that his or her contributions have been discounted. Such situations can happen in a direct way, such as when a team member's suggestions or ideas are rudely dismissed by other participants. It also can happen more subtly, such as when a team member's contributions are ignored or passed over without comment. Of course, irrelevant or unuseful ideas and opinions always will present challenges to the progress of a team. The response to such comments should not denigrate the speaker, however. Instead, the black belt should try to foster an environment in which team members gently can indicate why a particular idea won't work. Not only does this response show respect to the speaker, it gives him or her some extra insight into the project.

Avoiding Attributing Negative Motives to Other People

In a Six Sigma project team, poor communication has a compounding effect: when team members fail to interact honestly, they begin to misunderstand each other and then communication becomes even worse. If team members begin to attribute negative motives to one another, the effect on the team can be poisonous. The black belt or project leader always should be on the alert for this type of behavior. Whenever a team member makes assumptions about why another person is doing or not doing something, these assumptions are symptoms of poor communication. The response should be to call a meeting and address the nature of the disagreement. Team members should be responsible for explaining the reasons for their actions to colleagues. Six Sigma is an empirical, fact-based discipline, and this emphasis extends to the interactions among team members. The members of a Six Sigma team always should confirm the reasons for decisions and as much as possible should base their actions on information available to every member of the team.

Avoiding Rush to Accomplishment

Six Sigma is a program for success, but it does not produce instant results. Too often, team members are impatient during the course of a project, and they make mistakes in their rush to accomplishment. To keep this from happening, a black belt needs to be conservative when establishing the preliminary schedule. It is tempting to think that a team can be unprecedentedly fast and efficient, but setting unrealistic expectations can destroy morale. The success of a Six Sigma program relies on strict adherence to protocol, and the only way to ensure this adherence is to maintain a close watch on team members. Although checklists generally are not used in Six Sigma, they can be a good way to make sure that every step is taken on the road to project completion. When the black belt senses that a strong hunger for success among the members of the team, he or she may assign those members some easy tasks to provide that feeling of accomplishment.

Keeping Groups from Floundering

Depsite the specific protocol for moving through Six Sigma projects, many teams have a hard time getting started or finishing. Different reasons can cause this trouble, depending on when it occurs in the project. If the team has trouble getting started, often they are unsure of the scope or purpose of their efforts. Such a sense of uncertainty indicates that the black belt and sponsor have done a poor job of composing or publicizing the project charter. In such instances, the black belt should intervene and ensure that all team members understand what they are about to begin. If a team flounders in the middle of the project, usually data has been analyzed insufficiently, so the appropriate path forward is not evident to all team members. If the team flounders at the end of the project, effective contingency plans for making adjustments likely have not been conceived.

Handling Overbearing Group Members

Hierarchies exist within a Six Sigma team, and sometimes senior members can run roughshod over their subordinates. Besides being rude, however, this behavior is bad for the team because it alienates people and makes them less likely to share their ideas or commit fully to their work. When appropriate for one member of the team to have authority, such as when the team is dealing with that member's area of expertise, the black belt should allow that member some extra power. However, the black belt must make sure that this dynamic does not extend into other areas of the project. Moreover, the black belt must never let any team member assert him or herself without the support of data. Expertise and determination are necessary qualities in Six Sigma, but they cannot be allowed to crowd out cooperation and communication.

Handling Dominant Team Members

An ideal Six Sigma team will contain driven, confident stakeholders. However, some team members will overstep these boundaries and begin to dominate their peers to the detriment of the team. If some members of the group talk too much, talk too much about themselves, or otherwise monopolize conversation, the black belt and other team members may need to intervene. Specific techniques can reduce the potential for dominant team members. For instance, some black belts apply nominal group technique, in which a vote determines the priority of agenda items. Another way to reduce domination by one group member is by subtly deflecting this behavior as it emerges. The black belt might ask the dominant team member to work individually on a separate part of the project or might redirect conversation.

Handling Reluctant Team Members

For a Six Sigma project to be successful, every team member must feel comfortable sharing his or her ideas and opinions. It can be a problem when shy team members never contribute to group discussions. There always will be introverted and quiet people, however, so there must be structures for eliciting their feedback. One easy way to enact such structures is for the black belt or meeting leader to question each member of the team directly during each meeting. These questions should be concrete and impossible to evade. It could be useful to give the shy team members a specific brief, which they are required to discuss at every meeting. The individual differences between team members should be respected, but they cannot be allowed to disrupt honest communication or the generation of good ideas from all members of the group.

Team Formation

Successful Six Sigma teams usually do not cooperate without conflict at the beginning. Indeed, most groups must pass through some conflict and reconciliation periods before they can work effectively. The trajectory of a team has been codified according to four stages: forming, storming, norming, and performing. In the forming stage, the members of the team are getting to know one another, and so for the most part they are on their best behavior. At this point, the team has not yet begun working seriously enough to inspire much conflict. In the second stage, storming, the team begins its work in earnest, and differences between the members begin to emerge. During this stage team members will begin to assume different roles. The team leader must exercise control during this stage so conflicts can be resolved beneficially. In the norming stage, the team members settle their differences and settle on compromises that make effective work possible. This stage is called "norming" because team members are agreeing to normative behavior for the group. In the performing stage, the team operates at an optimal level because members have learned to work together.

Team Leader

A team leader is responsible for establishing and maintaining protocol, the set of rules by which the team will operate. The team leader also is charged with continuously realigning the team's efforts with the original goals and objectives. A team often will need to review first principles in order to stay on track. A team leader also is responsible for handling any conflicts that should arise during the project. A team leader will be responsible for planning and administrating the team's meetings. The team leader must meet with stakeholders and project sponsors in order to keep them apprised of the group's progress. A team leader must work continuously to improve the team's performance, first by helping members brainstorm and then by refining solutions through the use of data analysis.

Effective Change Agents

Most people claim to embrace change, but few people actually do so. Employees typically are reluctant to give up their old habits. To be effective change agents, the members of a Six Sigma team must first acknowledge the importance of having all employees on board with changes. Change agents take conscious steps to increase buy-in, commitment, and participation. Buy-in may be lacking if the goals of the project are unclear. Employees are more likely to participate and conform when they see how the proposed solutions will benefit them personally. However, employees will be skeptical if they believe the project team has prejudices and preconceived solutions. If the project team does not communicate regularly with the employees, the employees will lose faith in the project. Finally, buy-in will be reduced if the project's goals are too diffuse. Having a number of small projects with single targets is better than one giant project with several targets.

Common Problems for Teams

Team dynamics can be rough, especially during the early stages of a Six Sigma project. In order for a team to thrive, the roles must be defined and appropriate. In some cases, roles will be assigned by the team leader. At other times, it will be better for team members to settle into roles as they become familiar with one another. This latter process usually entails some conflict at first. A team also will struggle if members are not held accountable for their actions. Accountability is the responsibility of the team leader. Teams should meet only when necessary but should stay in regular communication throughout a project. When meetings do occur, they often are hijacked by members who digress, go off on tangents, or rudely reject the ideas of others. This behavior should be stopped immediately by the team leader. A similar group problem is groupthink, in which the members of a team are reluctant to disagree or do not have enough experience to come up with alternate solutions. Groupthink can result from having too little expertise in a team.

Response to Conflict

Avoidance

Five basic responses to conflict exist. These responses include avoidance, accommodation, competition, collaboration, and compromise. Avoidance is the least cooperative and assertive way to resolve a conflict. If a person notices a conflict but fails to bring it up or pursue it, he or she is avoiding the conflict. This may seem an ineffective behavior in the business world, but in some situations, avoidance is the correct response to conflict. If the conflict is insignificant or the outcome is assured, avoidance may be the best approach. In other words, if there is no chance of getting one's way, it may be better to avoid a conflict. Avoidance may also be the correct response if tempers are already hot over some other issue. It may be preferable to avoid a conflict until the members of the team have settled down. Another time to avoid conflict is when the possible consequences of disagreement vastly outweigh the benefits of resolution. Finally, a team member may be justified in avoiding conflict if he or she feels other members of the team can do a better job of resolving the issue.

Accommodation

Accommodation is the suppression of one's own interests in order to serve the interests of another person may be served. Accommodation can be a valuable tool in conflict resolution, as long as it does not engender resentment. In some cases, it team members should accommodate one another. For instance, a team member always should accommodate if he or she recognizes personal error. Another time to accommodate is when the issue is clearly much more important to the other person. When an issue is trivial to one person in a disagreement, that person may be better off conceding the point and hoping for consideration in the future. Accommodation also is appropriate when the group is fragile and more conflict could be very damaging. Of course, excessive accommodation can inspire some members to dominate the team, and in some cases accommodation will lead the team to accept the incorrect solution.

Competition

One response to conflict is competition, wherein the conflicting parties do their best to win. As long as the competition is fair, it can be a great way to settle disputes and generate excellent work. Most people perform better when they feel they are up against a competitor. Competition can be as simple as civilized argument during a meeting. Using competition as a response to conflict is appropriate when some members of the team are undecided. A team member also should be ready to compete when an issue is vital to the success of the business. Competition is an appropriate response to conflicts that need a clear resolution. An objective form of competition settles a dispute for good. When competition is used to settle disputes, the team leader should ensure that team members are fair and nice to one another. Also, competition sometimes becomes a habit in a team, which can be detrimental to cooperation in the future.

Collaboration

Collaboration is the response to conflict wherein team members work together to find a solution. When two team members disagree, they may collaborate until they come up with a resolution they both support. Collaboration is an effective style of conflict resolution when both parties have good points. Collaboration also is appropriate when members of a team have different areas of expertise, and so it is a good idea to combine their perspectives. Collaboration works when the conflicting parties have some personal disharmony; the process of collaborating may help them work through these problems. Collaboration also is a good idea when cooperation will increase buy-in from other team members and stakeholders. One problem with collaboration is that it can take a long time. For this reason, it should not be used to resolve unimportant conflicts. Also, collaboration can make room for too many viewpoints, which is a problem when some members of the team are inexpert.

Compromise

Compromise is a useful response to conflict when maintaining team harmony is more important than coming up with the best possible solution. Compromise, therefore, is not the right approach to ending crucial conflicts. It is appropriate, however, when two important members of the group are diametrically opposed on a key issue. If neither of these parties will give ground, a compromise may be the only way for the group to move forward. Compromise also can be the best course when no time exists for a lengthy debate or collaboration. Compromises can be very successful, but they sometimes leave the participants with lingering regrets. Also, compromises may produce mish-mash solutions that fail in the long run. Some problems require a clear, unified approach, and cannot be resolved through compromise. Finally, compromise should be avoided when it will disillusion some members of the team.

Histograms

A histogram is a tool for presenting data pictorially. It looks like a standard bar graph, except that each bar represents the total number of observations that lie within a range of ranked values. Histograms may be used during the measure and analyze stages of DMAIC. In these stages, histograms are useful for identifying multiple distributions for applying a distribution to capability analysis. Histograms are created by first placing all data in order from least to greatest. The number of bars in a histogram should equal the square root of the total set of data values. The width of each bar is the quotient of the range of data and the number of bars. The range of the data is calculated by subtracting the minimum value from the maximum value. Next, one should determine the number of data observations in each bar. The horizontal axis of the histogram will indicate the data values for each bar, and the vertical axis will indicate the number of observations.

Interpretation

Histograms effectively pinpoint the process location and variation. Histograms also indicate when data is symmetrical or bounded. A symmetrical distribution is characterized by data spread evenly about the histogram's center in an arrangement similar to a bell curve. If the histogram is more skewed, the data is not distributed evenly. For instance, if the data has more than one peak, it may have been obtained from multiple sources. A histogram only indicates the performance of the process as it is being measured. If the sample period was extended, the output would be considerably broader. Also, histograms do not take the sequence of the points into account, so they must be accompanied by measures of statistical process control. It is important to use a control chart to identify statistical control before fitting a distribution.

Pareto Charts

A Pareto chart is a form of bar graph in which problems are ranked according to their urgency. Each of the categories represented along the horizontal axis of a Pareto chart are exclusive, meaning that no single issue can fit into multiple categories. This characteristic is important because the category distinctions on a Pareto chart are largely subjective. Pareto charts are used during the define and analyze stages of DMAIC to guide the dispersal of resources and time to the most important issues. The categories on a Pareto chart are organized in descending order from left to right, according to whatever metric is deemed most appropriate. Most experts recommend that the metric be related either to count or to cost. Percentages and rates are not valid metrics for a Pareto chart.

Creation

The first step in creating a Pareto chart involves identifying the correct categories. These categories should be non-overlapping and fungible. The count/cost metric will be along the left axis of the chart, and the identities of the categories will be along the bottom axis. Data should be collected over the same interval for each category. The categories will be placed in descending order from left to right. An indication of the percent demarcations, or the percent of total cost/count represented by each variable, will run along the right vertical axis. The cumulative percentages from each bar are indicated with a line ascending from left to right. This cumulative aspect of the Pareto chart makes percentages and rates unacceptable as data. In order for the chart to work, the data must be additive.

Interpretation

Pareto charts attempt to isolate the categories that contribute the most to count or cost. In addition, the cumulative line aspect of the chart indicates the degree to which resolving problems with the most pressing issues would improve performance. The traditional method for using a Pareto chart involves identifying the left-most categories that approximate 80% of the count or cost. These categories are the most important areas. A Pareto chart with a steep cumulative line is better because in such a chart, the value is concentrated in the left-most categories. A relatively flat cumulative bar is less helpful, because this arrangement indicates no problems as more important than the rest. When a Pareto chart is flat, the categories have been subdivided too much. In such instances, regrouping into a few large categories may bring about a better result.

Cause-and-Effect Diagrams

Cause-and effect diagrams, sometimes known as fishbone or Ishikawa diagrams, are an easy and effective way to depict the reasons for a particular event. The typical layout of a cause-and-effect chart features the causes and effects listed in distinct boxes with arrows pointing from causes to effects. A cause *can* have more than one effect, and an effect *can* have more than one cause. Cause-and-effect diagrams are used during the analyze and improve stages of DMAIC. In the analyze stage, they are used to create innovative lists of possible process factors to be explored further in a designed experiment. In the improve stage, cause-and-effect diagrams are used to create lists of possible failure modes that must be considered when crafting a solution.

Creation and Interpretation

The first step in creating a cause-and-effect diagram is making a provisional list of the possible relationships between the process and the outcome. Phrasing the target in terms of a problem is better than phrasing the problem in terms of a goal. All of the factors that influence a main problem will branch off from that main problem. For some problems, beginning with either the four Ps (people, plants, policy, and procedures) or the 5Ms and E (measurement, material, methods, machines, manpower, and environment) will be appropriate. Using these models can ensure that no significant influences are overlooked. The main causes should be connected to the problem, and subordinate clauses should be connected to the main causes. In especially detailed diagrams, several hierarchical levels of causes may exist. Cause-and-effect diagrams are primarily brainstorming tools, not final assessments, so it is important to include many different possible answers. Once all of the causes and effects have been outlined, the group should examine the diagram to see whether certain categories exhibit a preponderance of causes. These categories may require further subdividing, or they may become targets for problem-solving efforts.

Scatter Diagrams

A scatter diagram is a simple plot on two axes, useful for investigating the correlation between two variables. Scatter diagrams are used during the analyze stage of DMAIC. The *x*-axis of a scatter diagram measures the independent variable (is the variable manipulated in the experiment) and the *y*-axis measures the dependent variable (the variable not manipulated in the experiment). The general method of an experiment involves making small adjustments to the independent variable and observing the effects on the dependent variable. The independent variable should be manipulated throughout the entire region of interest, so data points achieve sufficient spread on the diagram. Also, the data used on a scatter diagram should be generated especially for that purpose. Experimenters should be cautious when one variable appears to change along with another, since correlation does not imply causation. Perceived correlations suggest a need for further experimentation.

Nominal Group Technique

Nominal group technique (NGT) is a system for ranking non-objective data and is used primarily to create consensus or agreement in groups. Nominal group technique is used most commonly during the define and analyze stages of DMAIC. In the define stage, it is used to simplify project loads by combining redundant projects and eliminating unnecessary projects. In the analyze stage, nominal group technique helps teams agree on which solutions should be pursued. The first step in nominal group technique is to distribute paper to each team member. In the event of more than 35 options, each team member should receive eight pieces of paper; if there are 20 to 35 options, each member should receive six pieces of paper; and if there are less than 20 options, each member should receive four pieces of paper. Following discussion, each team member will select one option for each piece of paper he or she has received and indicate the option's rank on the paper. Then the papers are collected, and the weighted rankings are tabulated. The group then can focus on the most important and preferred options.

Identification of Sponsors in Project Charter

A project charter must identify the project's sponsors, or the managers who will provide guidance. The sponsors will provide funding to the project, give the team members access to resources, and inform other managers about the project's existence and intentions. One of the sponsor's jobs is to create enthusiasm and support for the project, so the project will receive any possible assistance from other employeesAs a result, the charter should identify appropriate sponsors. The sponsors should be selected from the departments most relevant to the project. In cases where the project participants are drawn from a number of different departments, the sponsors may need to be drawn from the ranks of those managers who oversee multiple departments. Such selection will make it possible for the project team to receive all the required support. Also, team members should avoid selecting sponsors who are already involved in several other projects.

Identification of Stakeholders and Team Members in Project Charter

A project charter should identify the stakeholders as clearly as possible. Stakeholders are all of the people and groups affected by the problem being addressed and potentially affected by the project as it progresses. In Six Sigma, the team should use a top-level process map to identify all of the affected groups. Affected groups may include customers, suppliers, other employees, and specific departments within the organization. The charter also should identify the members of the project team, or all the stakeholders participating in the project. Most projects are headed up by a single black belt, with one or more green belts representing each relevant department. Some projects may require the participation of experts or skilled employees. In rare cases, a Six Sigma project team will include a facilitator to ensure that all members of the team work together effectively.

Define Phase

Stage Objectives

The method for problem solving in Six Sigma is expressed as the acronym DMAIC, which stands for define, measure, analyze, improve, and control. The first state, define, focuses on identifying and articulating a project's important characteristics, including identification of the goals, objectives, and scope of the project. The Six Sigma team also should make explicit the team members and sponsors, as well as the proposed schedule for the project. The Six Sigma team should define the desired result of the project, otherwise known as the deliverable. In considering the process to be improved, the team should identify the stakeholders, the input/output structure, and the functions involved. The other component of the define stage is selecting and assembling a team able to accomplish all of the proposed goals. The members of this team must be able to work together well and must all have a solid understanding of the task before them. Moreover, all the members of the team should agree with the desirability of successfully completing the project.

Project Charter

Benefits

A project charter is an overview of the project. It changes as the project moves along, so team members and sponsors will remain on the same page. Management should approve the project charter in order to give the project legitimacy and informed guidance. A good project charter will establish clear deliverables, so its success or failure can be measured. Also, a good project charter will direct employee efforts to the right areas because it will identify the key variables that affect performance at all levels. A project charter will ensure that a proposed project does not interfere with other work performed in the company, because it will make public the intentions of the team. The project charter also will ensure that Six Sigma efforts are directed to the most important aspects of performance, and that they deal with processes integral to the business in the future.

Project Statement, Scope, and Deliverables

The project charter is a document in which the most important details about the project are codified. Of course, this document will be subject to revision as necessary. One of the hallmarks of the DMAIC structure, and indeed of Six Sigma itself, is a willingness to rethink first principles at any time. The first step in composing an effective project charter is to make the problem statement explicit. The team should ask itself why the project is necessary. The reasons clearly should be integral to the optimal function of the business. Indeed, a project charter should express deliverable in terms of actual output and in a manner approved by the financial department of the organization. In most cases, it is necessary to confirm the reasonableness of the estimate with the finance department before writing it into the charter. The charter also should include a reasonable estimation of the project scope, based on the data collected thus far.

Schedule, Stakeholders, and Team Composition

A project charter must include a provisional schedule. This schedule should include specific dates on which established objectives and goals are to be met. Although the schedule established at the beginning of a project is unlikely to survive the imposition of unforeseen events, project leaders should be as specific and prudent as possible. The project charter also should include a complete identification of the stakeholders in a project. Stakeholders are those persons who influence a project or are affected by a project. Along with an identification of the stakeholders, a project charter should include a list of the team members. Of course, the list of stakeholders and team members will feature significant overlap.

Finalizing

A project charter should include an appointment for an initial meeting, at which the team members will discuss and consent to the scope, deliverables, and provisional schedule to be included in the charter. This meeting allows team members to become acquainted with one another if they are not already and to voice any initial concerns or ideas related to the project. Having agreed upon the core items of the project, the team should map the top level of the process to be improved. This information should be entered into a new, updated version of the charter, which then should be submitted to the sponsor for approval. Obtaining this approval is important so both project participants and sponsors understand the nature of the work about to be undertaken. This way, any initial misgivings can be addressed without much loss of resources.

Problem Statement

A project charter typically will begin with a problem statement in which the author defines an adverse situation in the business, or the target of the proposed project. If possible, a problem statement should provide measurable evidence of the problem's existence. It also should describe the problem in terms of poor outputs. The collection of objective data related to the problem may not be easy, particularly if the problem relates to a new business process or a process previously not addressed. However, the project charter should include as much preliminary data as possible, with the understanding that it will be updated as the project moves along and more data becomes available. The measure stage of the DMAIC model is an opportunity for the team to refine its charter through direct acquisition of data. The presence of objective data is important because it justifies the decision to direct resources toward the project.

Defining Business Need to Be Addressed

A project charter needs to identify the specific business need or needs that will be addressed by the proposed project. In other words, the charter must name the business processes that will be improved by the successful completion of the project. As with the problem statement, this section of the charter should include as much objective data as possible. It may be difficult for the author to estimate the value of the project to specific business processes, particularly if this estimate is based on minimal and preliminary data in the problem statement. However, if possible the charter should refer to specific metrics such as the number of defects, schedule, or profit. Many Six Sigma theorists recommend that all projects have a clear and measurable benefit to the customer. Comprehensive project charters will address business needs related to the customer, stakeholders, and other employees.

Statement of Objective and Identification of Resources

A complete project charter should include a statement of objective in which the author provides a definition for the intended result of the project. Most Six Sigma experts recommend expressing this result in financial terms, since such terms are easy to understand and unlikely to vary. Other measures, like defects per million or return on investment, may be used but are more subject to variation and unforeseen influences. A complete project charter also will identify the resources required for the project. The efforts and time of the team members are not included in this summary. The resources may include equipment, materials, computer time, databases, and other employees. The resources required by a project are not only those resources necessary to improve the process, but also those necessary to collect and analyze data along the way.

Project Scope

A project charter will include a clear description of the project scope, or the particular part of the problem to be targeted. For a number of reasons, it is better for projects to have a limited scope. Otherwise, objectives can become team members can become disgruntled, and resources can be wasted when a project stretches out indefinitely. In general, Six Sigma projects should take no more than four months. Longer projects run the risk of losing key members. If the members of a team have a vision that cannot be realized within four months, they should consider whether the grand project might be divided into multiple smaller projects. Indeed, the composition of the charter is an excellent time to consider the appropriate scale for team efforts. Often, a team will decide to solve a particular problem, only to discover that it depends on a collection of smaller problems that must be resolved first. In such a case, the team may want to conduct a series of smaller projects rather than grouping the entire problem in one project.

Deliverables

A project charter should include a clear and measurable identification of the deliverables created by the project. A deliverable is any fungible benefit or advantage. Identifying deliverables is important because it enables the overall success or failure of the project to be assessed. Establishing targets for deliverables allows the project to be judged on its own terms. One common mistake is to list aspects of the project's method as deliverables. For instance, some project charters will identify the data obtained during the project as a deliverable. This is misguided, in part because the data would not be necessary if not for the existence of the project. Although systems such as statistical process control have utility for an organization beyond the scope of the project in which they are created, they should not be counted as deliverables. If possible, deliverables should be placed in financial terms.

Schedule

A project charter should include some form of schedule, even if the schedule likely will be modified once the project begins. The schedule should include the date on which the charter was approved by the sponsor as well as the start and completion dates. A good charter will indicate the dates on which each phase of the DMAIC schedule will be complete. This process is known as a phase-gate review. The authors of the charter will use critical path or program evaluation and review technique (PERT) analysis to set the target dates. The schedule typically is expressed as a Gantt chart, in which each phase of the project is defined, and the prerequisites and required resources are listed. Each of the phases of the DMAIC schedule should be subdivided into a set of activities.

Project Status Report

Project status reports begin with a current schedule and brief description of the project. A project status report should include a list of the action items, or the tasks to be completed by assigned team members at particular times. The project status report also will include lists of roadblocks, or hindrances to progress not yet resolvable by specific actions. A project status report also will include a list of the data obtained during each phase of the project. Finally, the project status report should list any items that should have been finished but have not yet. These are called outstanding items. Project status reports typically are issued once or twice a week and every time one of the DMAIC phases is completed. Copies of the report are sent to the sponsor, team members, and any other relevant stakeholders.

Customer Requirements

Expression in Business-to-Business Transactions

In a business-to-business transaction, the buyer usually is very specific about product or service requirements. Typically the customer expresses a nominal value, or target, accompanied by upper and lower specifications. In other words, the customer declares the value he or she would prefer and then indicates the range of values he or she would tolerate. Any delivered products that fall outside this range are defective and will be returned. Defective products create waste for the customer and the supplier, alike. A supplier who consistently delivers defective products soon will be replaced. However, suppliers should not focus exclusively on the specification values expressed by customers, as such a focus gives a warped view of the customer's requirements. Instead, the supplier should focuson meeting the customer's stated requirements and looking for ways to add more value.

Expression in Business-to-Customer Transactions

In business-to-customer (B2C) transactions, the business usually has less information about the customer requirements than in a B2B transaction. Moreover, significant variations in customer requirements may exist. Some customers may have different requirements depending on other factors such as time of day or physical location. Collecting information about customers in B2C transactions is time consuming and potentially expensive, but it gives the business the opportunity to micro-target market segments. That is, a business can take the information it gathers to develop small-scale marketing strategies for specific customers and potential customers. In a B2C transaction, customer requirements may not be expressed directly or explicitly. However, they may be just as objective and susceptible to appeal as those of a customer in a B2B transaction.

Gantt Charts

Gantt charts are used to identify the critical path of each dependent task in a particular project. The critical path includes everything that has to be done to maintain the project's timing. Any process not on the critical path may be slightly delayed without extending the overall duration of the project. These activities are said to have built-in slack time. At the beginning of a Six Sigma project, distinguishing the tasks that are on the critical path is important. The use of Gantt charts typically is restricted to the define stage of DMAIC. The intention of this chart is to identify those tasks that, if truncated, would lead to an overall cycle time reduction. In addition, a comprehensive Gantt chart will make it possible to place all project activities on the schedule. In some cases, a Gantt chart may be used during the improve stage to confirm the reduction of critical path cycle time.

Creation

Gantt charts are useful for identifying the critical path of a process. The first step in the creation of a Gantt chart is to make a list of all the tasks that have to be completed in the project. After these tasks have been placed in the order in which they need to be performed, it should be determined whether some tasks may be performed simultaneously or whether some tasks require the completion of previous steps before they may be initiated. On a Gantt chart, jobs that can be done at the same time are placed on parallel paths, and other jobs are placed in sequence. Within each parallel path, there may be serial tasks. However, if one of the parallel paths can be completed more quickly than another, then some slack time can be built in to that path.

Interpretation

Gantt charts help businesses create the fastest-possible schedule for a process. The most important benefit of a Gantt chart is that it indicates areas within the process that can tolerate lag. Essentially, a process that is not on the critical path may be initiated a little late or finished a little early. For every task, though, there will be some time by which it must be initiated and some time by which it must be finished. Of course, it is not always possible to obtain a precise measure for the duration of a particular task. For this task, it may be necessary to perform program evaluation and review techniques (PERT) analysis. PERT analysis can gauge the probability of a task being completed within a certain amount of time.

Affinity Diagrams

Affinity diagrams organize a collection of issues, problems, or ideas so they may be utilized effectively. The diagram is so called because it identifies the affinities, or similarities, between seemingly disparate ideas or problems. Organizations using affinity diagrams often discover unforeseen relationships between variables. These diagrams often are used at the beginning of a process, when the team is trying to gain a primary understanding of the problem. An affinity diagram can be useful for building a consensus when members of a team have divergent interests and knowledge bases. However, affinity diagrams may be used in every phase of the DMAIC process. One common result of an affinity diagram is the identification and elimination of redundancies in thinking.

Creation

To create an affinity diagram, teams begin by identifying the target issue or problem. The next step is to have each member of the team list a few issues that impact this target. It is important to collect as many ideas as possible. Once the ideas are collected into a general list, they can be organized into categories. Redundant items may be discarded. Discussion or even argument about the logic of sorting is typical. The team leader should administer this part of the process calmly and proactively. Once the categories have been labeled and filled, the group should come up with header cards for each title. The titles may be useful for nominal group technique or in the creation of a prioritization matrix. If the process is a success, then the main ideas listed on the header cards will indicate the most important drivers to be addressed for the achievement of objectives and goals. It should be noted that affinity diagrams do not require objective information; instead, these diagrams are tools for organizing the subjective impressions of team members.

SIPOC

SIPOC (suppliers, inputs, processes, outputs, and customers) analysis provides a comprehensive look at a process. SIPOC is used during the define stage of DMAIC, when the Six Sigma team tries to identify each top-level process, as well as its stakeholders. In the context of SIPOC analysis, suppliers are those persons who contribute inputs to the process. Inputs are defined as all of the knowledge, resources, and information required to produce the desired output. A process is defined as any task that translates inputs into outputs. Accordingly, the outputs are the deliverables, or the products of the process. Finally, the customers are all of those parties that receive the deliverables (outputs). SIPOC is initiated with the creation of a flowchart or process map. Typically, the first category to be identified is the outputs. From there, locating the customers, inputs, and suppliers will be easier.

Work Breakdown Structures

A work breakdown structure is a diagram that depicts the parts of a problem or process. These diagrams are useful when a problem seems overwhelming, because they break the problem down into manageable "sub-problems." Work breakdown structures are most useful during the define and analyze stages of DMAIC. In the define stage, work breakdown structures are combined with Pareto analysis to organize problems before solutions are applied. A work breakdown structure also may be useful at this time to eliminate less important areas of a project and thereby ensure adherence to a schedule. In the analyze stage, work breakdown structures are used to organize all of the issues and complaints to be handled during the improve stage. The completion of a work breakdown structure often suggests that different solutions should be applied to different parts of a general problem.

Creation and Interpretation

A work breakdown structure is created first by breaking a problem into components. Each component of the problem subsequently should be broken down into categories. These categories should represent the different ways the particular problem can occur. The intention of the work breakdown structure is to reduce complex problems to a collection of discrete and manageable issues. The organization of a complex situation creates a map for problem solving that can be used by members of different departments. A comprehensive and effective work breakdown structure will create material for other data-organization charts such as Pareto charts. The information displayed on a work breakdown structure would be prioritized on the resulting Pareto chart.

Matrix Diagrams

Matrix diagrams indicate the relationships between several items in multiple groups. A matrix diagram is a table in which the value in each cell indicates the strength of the relationship. Matrix diagrams often are used during the define and improve stages of DMAIC. In the define stage, these diagrams are used to pick projects that will contribute to the achievement of organizational objectives and goals. Also, matrix diagrams can be used in the define and improve stages to examine the similarity between customer desires and process metrics. The first step in the creation of a matrix diagram is to identify the items for comparison. Six Sigma teams often transfer the categories from some other chart, such asan affinity diagram. The next step is to use consensus decision-making rules to evaluate the relationships between each pair of values. In this subjective process, the team should perform carefully and according to an organized protocol.

Measure Phase

Process Metrics

Identification

One of the key tasks of the measure stage is to identify process metrics. Typically, quite a few process metrics can provide useful information about a particular process. These metrics tend to relate to schedule, cost, or quality. Factors critical to schedule (CTS) have a direct bearing on the completion date of the process. Factors critical to quality (CTQ) have a direct effect on the desired characteristics of the product or service. Factors critical to cost (CTC) have an impact on materials, labor, delivery, overhead, inventory, and/or the cost to the consumer of the good or service. As much as possible, these metrics should be customer-focused and transparent: that is, they should provide immediate objective data that can be analyzed. Moreover, these metrics need to be obtained with measurement systems that are repeatable and reproducible.

Important Characteristics

Process metrics must be reliable, repeatable, and reproducible. Otherwise, they cannot be considered effective illustrations of process characteristics. At the same time, measurements must be specific and detailed enough to distinguish between the effects of process alterations and process noise. As much as possible, metrics should relate to actual targets of business strategy and should result from cooperation between employees. Before any metrics are applied, employees from several different departments should judge them. If possible, metrics should be related to actual services provided to customers. Finally, metrics should pertain to values critical to quality, schedule, or cost, as these factors are the three most important variables in any process.

Critical-to-Quality Metrics

One of the more common critical-to-quality metrics is yield, or the amount of completed product divided by the amount of product that began the process. Obviously, a business would like to have yield equal 1 (or 100%). The difference between perfection and reality is known as the scrap rate. If a process had a yield of 95%, the scrap rate would be 5%. Yield is a useful metric, although it does not indicate where in the process errors occurred. Also, yield does not distinguish those pieces of scrap that can still be salvaged. A slightly more advanced metric is throughput yield, or the average percentage of units with no defects. When multiple steps in a process are considered, Six Sigma teams use rolled throughput yield, which measures the expected quality level after several steps.

Regression Analysis

Regression analysis is a system for identifying when independent variables are influenced by one or more dependent variables. Regression analysis may be used during the measure, analyze, and improve stages of DMAIC. In the measure stage, regression analysis is used to evaluate the degree to which a measurement system is linear. During the analyze stage, regression analysis can be used to explore the connections between metrics and process factors. In the improve stage, regression analysis is useful for confirming these connections after improvements have been implemented. A scatter diagram often is interpreted with a simple linear regression analysis. If more than one factor influences the value of the independent variable, then multiple regression is necessary.

Residuals Analysis

Residuals are the differences between a response's observed value and a regression model's predicted value for that response. A residuals analysis of a regression model will reveal any unusual patterns that could suggest error in the model. In statistical terms, this is expressed $e_i = y_i - \hat{y}_i$.

Statistical software programs such as Excel will calculate a standardized residual $e_i/\sqrt{s^2}$, such that the variance is set to 1. This makes outliers more obvious. Perhaps the most common technique of residuals analysis is the normality test, in which the randomness of error is tested by creating a distribution of the residuals. If the error truly is random, then the residuals should follow a normal distribution with a mean of zero. Residuals also can be used on a scatter diagram to assess the independence of a variable.

EWMA Charts

An exponentially weighted moving average (EWMA) charge is a type of control charge primarily used for variables data. The creator of the chart selects a weighting factor, which assigns different values to data depending on its age. This type of chart uses data from every available sample, so it can identify extremely small variations in the process. Exponentially weighted moving-average charts are used during the measure and control stages of DMAIC. In the measure stage, these charts are used to baseline a process. Exponentially weighted moving-average charts are valuable especially for this purpose when the process might be nonnormal and the rational subgroup size is only one. In the control stage, exponentially weighted moving-average charts are used to control the process, either for the reasons outlined in the measure stage or when it is necessary to detect extremely small shifts in the process. Given the same sample size, an exponentially weighted moving average chart can detect shifts from 1/2σ to 2σ faster than a Shewhart chart.

One of the most important initial steps in the creation of an exponentially weighted moving-average chart is setting the value for λ (lambda), the weighting factor. To detect small shifts, the value should be set around 0.2; to detect large shifts, the value should be set between 0.2 and 0.4. The plotted statistic for an EWMA is calculated with $z_t = \lambda_1 \bar{x}_t + (1 - \lambda_1) z_{t-1}$, where *t* is a particular time, λ is the value of the weighting factor, $\bar{x}_t$ is the subgroup average for the present subgroup at t, and the value of *z* at t_0 is either the overall average or a target. The control limits are calculated with $\text{CL}_{\text{EWMA}} = z_0 \pm \left(\frac{3\bar{R}}{d_2\sqrt{n}}\right)\sqrt{\frac{\lambda}{(2-\lambda)}[1-(1-\lambda)^{2t}]}$, where z_0 is the target value or process mean value, *n* is the size of the subgroup, *m* is the number of functions being analyzed, and d_2 is a function of *n*.

Interpretation

The first step in the interpretation of exponentially weighted moving-average charts is to examine the range chart. If this chart is out of statistical control, then the control limits found on the EWMA cannot be trusted. Any points out of statistical control should be linked to special causes of variation. The team may need to think creatively in order to discover the sources of process variation. After the range chart has been reviewed, the EWMA chart may be compared to the control limits. Run tests and specifications are irrelevant in the interpretation of EWMA charts, because process observations will display much broader variation. If the process appears to be stable, then it considering its capability relative to requirements may be useful.

R & R Analysis

Gauge repeatability and reproducibility (R & R) analysis assigns a numerical value to the errors caused by a particular measurement system. Gauge repeatability and reproducibility analysis is used most often during the measure and control stages of DMAIC. In the measure stage, this analysis generally is used to assess the degree to which measurement error contributes to common- and special-cause variation in estimates of process baseline. It also can be used in this stage to confirm gauge discrimination. In the control stage, gauge repeatability and reproducibility analysis is used to evaluate the accuracy of specific measurement systems. The success of an R & R analysis depends on the collection of representative samples. A measurement system cannot be evaluated correctly except by its performance with respect to typical samples.

PROCESS

When analyzing gauge repeatability and reproducibility (R & R), using samples obtained during actual operations is essential. Also, each appraiser should receive the samples in a random order, although someone other than the appraiser should be able to identify the samples. In a standard gauge repeatability and reproducibility analysis, there are three appraisers and ten samples: each appraiser measures each sample three times. However the test is arranged, there should be multiple trials for each sample in order for repeatability to be assessed. While a large sample size is preferable, this analysis can be expensive, which is a limiting factor. Again, it is essential to obtain a representative sample so all the potential sources of variation in the process are evident.

INTERPRETATION OF DISCRIMINATION RATIOS AND GAUGE REPEATABILITY AND REPRODUCIBILITY

In gauge repeatability and reproducibility analysis, the discrimination ratio is an estimate of the number of different categories a measurement system can identify. In most cases, eight distinct categories are necessary before the measurement system can be subjected to statistical analysis. The gauge repeatability and reproducibility statistic typically is expressed as a percentage of total process variation or as a percentage of tolerance. If reported as a percentage of process variation, it suggests how useful the measurement system will be in process capability analysis and control charting. If reported as a percentage of tolerance, it suggests how useful the process will be for determining the acceptability of the process deliverables. If the measurement system error is large relative to tolerance, there is a greater chance of improperly accepting or rejecting output. For both tolerance and process variation, a percentage from 0 to 10% is acceptable, while a percentage of more than 30% is unacceptable.

ANALYSIS OF VARIANCE

In an analysis of variance, variation within each subgroup is compared to the variation found between different subgroups. The variation within each subgroup is found by sampling from the subgroup repeatedly. The variation between different subgroups is found by analyzing the essential differences between the averages of each subgroup. Analysis of variance begins with the null hypothesis, that all subgroup averages are equal. Then, the F statistic is used to compare the average variation between subsets, known as the mean square treatment, with the sun of the squares of the residuals, known as the mean square error. An F test assumes that subsets have a normal distribution and equal variance. If the p value for the F test is less than 0.05, then the null hypothesis can be rejected. This suggests that one or more of the subset averages is different.

ESTIMATION OF CONFIDENCE INTERVAL ON MEAN

One of the more useful forms of statistical inference is the estimation of confidence interval on mean, which requires a population sample. This technique can be useful during the measure and analyze stages of DMAIC. The use of this technique assumes that the sample represents the entire population and that it has a normal distribution. Also, the sample should be constant, meaning that it can be assumed to remain relatively stable through time. During the measure stage, an estimation of confidence interval on mean is used to estimate the process average when a process control cannot be set because of a lack of data. This process average is used for baseline estimates. In the analyze stage, an estimation of the confidence interval on mean is used to examine the similarities and differences between the sample means taken during various process conditions.

Process When Historical Standard Deviation is Known

When the historical standard deviation is known, the process of estimating the confidence interval on the mean begins with calculating the average $\bar{X}$ for n sample units. The confidence interval may then be calculated with the following formula: $\bar{X} - Z_{\alpha/2}(\sigma/\sqrt{n}) < \mu < \bar{X} + Z_{\alpha/2}(\sigma/\sqrt{n})$. In this approach, it is assumed that the samples are taken from a population with a normal distribution. Therefore, the z values are calculated according to the confidence level. If the confidence level is 90%, then $\alpha = 0.1$. The confidence interval is two-sided: that is, it extends from one side of the mean to the other. Therefore, the α value is divided in two: $\alpha/2 = 0.05$. The z value, then, can be obtained by referring to a chart of areas under the normal curve.

Process When Historical Standard Deviation is Unknown

In some cases, the historical standard deviation is unknown, and so an alternate method for estimating the confidence interval on the mean must be used. First, one must calculate the average $\bar{X}$ and the sample standard deviation s for n sample units. The confidence interval is calculated with the formula $\bar{X} - t_{\alpha/2,n-1}(s/\sqrt{n}) < \mu < \bar{X} + t_{\alpha/2,n-1}(s/\sqrt{n})$. As with a known historical standard deviation, it is assumed that the samples are taken from a population with a normal distribution. Again, the confidence interval will be two-sided, so confidence level should be divided by two. Confidence interval calculations can be executed in both Minitab and Excel, although in Minitab one must have the raw data in order to proceed.

Interpretation

An estimation of the confidence interval on the mean indicates the percentage of samples that will contain the true population mean, otherwise known as μ (mu). For example, if the confidence limit on the mean is estimated at 97%, one can expect that 97% of samples the confidence interval will include μ. The estimation of the true mean becomes more assured as the number of sampled increases. In other words, the confidence interval and the number of samples are inversely proportionate. This estimation is more powerful when the standard deviation, or σ, is known. When the standard deviation is unknown, the *t* tables must be used. When the standard deviation is known, the *z* tables may be used.

Confidence Interval on Proportion

In some cases, analysts will have a solid history of the standard deviation for a given population. In such cases, analysts can estimate the confidence level of the mean at a particular confidence level. This statistical technique can be useful during the measure and analyze stages of DMAIC. As with the confidence interval on mean, the sample being used must represent the entire population, must be constant, and must have a normal distribution. In the measure stage, this technique is useful in situations where limited data exists for the purposes of establishing a process control. In such a case, estimations of the confidence interval on proportion can be used to estimate the average error rates for processes.

Process of Estimation

To estimate the confidence interval on proportion, begin by calculating the average error rate $\hat{p}$ for n sample units. The confidence interval is then calculated with the formula

$\hat{p} - Z_{\alpha/2}\sqrt{\frac{\hat{p}(1-\hat{p})}{n}} \leq p \leq \hat{p} + Z_{\alpha/2}\sqrt{\frac{\hat{p}(1-\hat{p})}{n}}$. As with estimate of the confidence interval on proportion, this operation assumes that the samples are taken from a population with a normal distribution.

Also, the confidence interval is two-sided, running from one side of the mean to the other. The z value can be obtained from a table that outlines areas under the standard normal curve.

Interpretation

The confidence interval on proportion indicates the percentage of samples in which the confidence interval will include the true error rate. For example, if the confidence limit on the error rate is calculated as 90%, it may be assumed that nine out of ten samples will include the true error rate if the confidence interval is reached. As with the interval on the mean, the confidence interval on proportion decreases as the number of samples increases. In other words, when more samples are obtained, fewer values are required to create confidence. The opposite is true, as well: when the number of samples is small, a larger confidence interval is required. Process stability cannot be determined simply by the fact that a particular sample falls within the confidence interval. Process stability must be confirmed with a statistical process control chart.

Linearity Analysis

Linearity analysis judges the possibility that the bias error found in a particular system of measurement will be present throughout the equipment's entire operating range. It is important to know whether a measurement system can be trusted for large as well as small values. Linearity analysis often is used during the measure stage of DMAIC. In this stage, linearity analysis is useful for assessing the accuracy of a measurement system within the range of values likely to be observed during the process. The standard procedure for analyzing linearity was established by the Automotive Industry Action Group. The first step selecting multiple parts to examine throughout the operating range. A reference value should be obtained with precise equipment. The next step is having different employees measure the parts throughout the range with the intended measurement system. The average of these measurements should be found, and then the bias can be calculated by subtracting the average measurement from the reference value. This data then should be depicted on a scatter diagram. The adequacy of the measurement system is assessed using R^2, the coefficient of determination. A value of greater than 70% is acceptable in most cases.

Matrix Diagrams

A few different types of matrix diagrams exist, each of which may be useful in particular circumstances. In a directional system, arrows suggest the nature of the relationship between each pair of items. Sophisticated directional systems have weighted arrows that indicate the direction of causation as well as the importance. In a numerical matrix diagram, numbers perform the same functions as weighted arrows. For example, on a ten-point scale a 5 might indicate a moderate relationship in one direction, while a 1/5 indicates a moderate relationship in the opposite direction. In a plus-minus system, a plus sign indicates a relationship and a minus sign indicates the absence of a relationship. In a symbol system, finally, triangles, circles, and squares indicate characteristics of each relationship. Matrix diagrams typically have final rows and columns that tally up the total importance of each item or process. The team then can identify the items and processes that have the most significance.

Process

The first major step in the measure stage is to create a comprehensive process level map of processes as currently performed. In other words, during this stage the group defines and clearly describes all of the activities they aim to improve. This is a much more detailed and comprehensive version of the top-level process map created in the define stage. A detailed process map typically requires the participation of expert employees. This participation is important especially because employees may have a vastly different conception of process sequence than their superiors. Often, employees will have streamlined or modified a process without notifying management. Judging the beneficiality of customizations made by employees is unnecessary and potentially harmful. The primary concern at this point is to create an accurate map of the process as currently performed.

FLOWCHARTS

A flowchart is a basic tool for recording all of the steps in a particular process. Flowcharts are used during the measure, analyze, improve, and control stages of DMAIC. In the measure stage, flowcharts can be used to map a process as it is currently being performed or to identify how different shareholders perceive a particular process or problem. In the analyze stage, a flowchart can be used to identify complications in a process that can lengthen cycle time or cause adverse variations. In the improve stage, flowcharts can be used to diagram possible improvements and changes. Finally, in the control stage, flowcharts can be used to map out processes that have been revised and improved.

CREATION AND INTERPRETATION

Flowcharts simplify communication by representing each task in a sequence with a symbol. Most organizations endorse the use of the symbols created by the American National Standards Institute. Some employees already will be familiar with the ANSI system, in which decisions are represented by diamonds and processes are represented by rectangles. Some flowcharts will incorporate different colors to suggest departmental divisions and time distinctions. Flowcharts are fairly easy to interpret, assuming the team already is familiar with the process. One thing to look for is a preponderance of decision points, as this occurrence may lead to unnecessary delays or adverse variations. The goal of process improvement is to reduce complications and unnecessary lags. Therefore, the interpretation of a flowchart always should be performed with an eye toward simplifying as much as possible.

Analyze Phase

Primary Objectives

In the analyze stage of DMAIC, the Six Sigma team will focus on analyzing the sources of variation in the target process. This analysis may require the use of sophisticated statistical tools. The team also will analyze the value stream. The value stream is the set of activities that create value for the customer. During the analyze stage, the team will identify the process drivers, which are the activities that exert a significant influence on the results of processes. Obviously, the intention of the Six Sigma efforts will be to enhance those activities that add value and to eliminate those activities that take up time and resources without adding much value. The value stream only includes those activities necessary for the creation of the product or service. The judgment of value should be from the perspective of the customer rather than from the perspective of stakeholders within the company.

Value Stream Analysis

The value stream is the entire series of activities that create value in a product or service. The addition value is considered from the perspective of the customer rather than from the perspective of employees or management within the company. During process mapping, the Six Sigma team will divide the activities into three categories: value-added activities, business-value-added activities, and non-value-added activities. Value-added activities, as the name suggests, create value for the customer. Business-value-added (BVA) activities do not create value for the customer, but are necessary anyway. These activities sometimes are referred to as Type 1 waste. Some examples of BVA activities are marketing, design, and delivery. Non-value-added (NVA) activities create value for neither the customer nor the business. The goal of Six Sigma projects is to eliminate as many NVA activities as possible.

Identification of NVA Activities

Six Sigma teams use tools such as matrix diagrams and quality function deployment efforts to identify non-value-added activities. As always, the question of value should be considered from the customer's perspective. If an activity does not create something for which a customer would be willing to pay, it likely does not add value. One common form of NVA activity is improper or unsuccessful designs. When a business spends time and effort designing products or services that the customer ultimately rejects, then the business has failed to add value. If a business process contains some unnecessary or redundant steps, these steps are classified as NVA activities. Any work that does not translate into a product or service for the customer is considered NVA. For instance, inventory reorganization provides nothing to the customer, although it may be necessary at times. Any unnecessary transport of people or resources is considered NVA activity.

Control Charts to Identify Variation Sources

In the analyze stage of DMAIC, the Six Sigma team will look closely at the statistical control charts created during the measure stage. One of the initial goals of analysis will be to distinguish special and common causes of variation. Special causes of variation do not occur during every performance of the process, but when they do, they cause significant delay. On a control chart, special causes of variation will be indicated by points that lie far outside the normal range. The location of these out-of-control points will suggest possible sources of the variation. That is, it will be possible to see at which point during the process the variation occurred. Common causes of variation will influence each iteration of the process and therefore will not be obvious on a control chart. Several reasons for common cause variation may exist. Variations from common cause, then, may be more difficult to diagnose.

Process Cycle Efficiency Metric

The measurement of process cycle efficiency is used to determine the most useful and positive ways to improve cycle time. The process cycle efficiency metric is used most often during the analyze stage of DMAIC. The general method for calculating process cycle efficiency is to divide value-added time by process lead time. Process lead time is calculated by dividing the number of items in a process by the number of times the process is completed in an hour. This calculation is known as Little's law. A process can attain a maximum process cycle efficiency of 100% if all the activities in the process add value. However, it is more typical for processes to approach 25% efficiency after the implementation of lean strategies. The reasonable value for efficiency depends in large part on the type of activity. Creative activities usually have efficiency values of approximately 5%, although lean management strategies have been known to increase this figure up to almost 25%. Transactional activities, on the other hand, sometimes can reach efficiency values of up to 50%.

Binomial and Poisson Distributions

Binomial distributions are useful when the units in a population exist in only two states. For instance, if the only possible characteristics of a population are "off" and "on," a binomial distribution can be used to estimate the total number of "offs" and "ons" in a population. A binomial distribution only applies when trials are independent and the number of samples in the population is fixed. In a binomial distribution, the distributional parameter is the average proportion. This value is assumed or calculated by dividing the number of sample items that meet the condition by the total number of items in the sample. A Poisson distribution, on the other hand, can guess the number of times a particular condition will occur for a given process or population. The distinguishing feature of the Poisson distribution is its appropriateness for situations in which the targeted condition may occur more than once in each unit. The Poisson distribution accurately estimates the number of events in each sample unit. As with the binomial distribution, the trials be should be independent, and the data should be composed of positive whole numbers. In a Poisson distribution, the distributional parameter is the average number of instances per unit.

Normal Distributions

Normal distributions are used for continuous data that have neither an upper nor a lower boundary. A normal distribution looks like the classic bell curve. For a normal distribution, the average of a sample, $\bar{X}$, is calculated by adding all the measurements and dividing by the total number of measurements, N. The standard deviation of N is calculated with the following formula:

$$s = \frac{\sum_{j=1}^{N} (\bar{X} - X_1)^2}{N}$$

One must the calculate a z value so this particular standard deviation may be considered a standardized normal distribution with a standard deviation of 1 and a mean of zero. The z value is calculated with $z = \frac{(X - \bar{X})}{s}$. Once this z value is obtained, it is possible to estimate the likelihood of being greater or less than a particular value for x.

Hypothesis Testing

Hypothesis testing establishes a degree of confidence and then compares a sample statistic against a historical value or another sample statistic. In other words, hypothesis testing allows one to make statistical inferences about the characteristics of a population. This sort of testing is useful for distinguishing the factors that contribute to variation in data. Primarily, this type of testing is used during designed experiments and regression analysis. Hypothesis testing often is performed during the analyze and improve stages of DMAIC. In the improve stage, its primary function is comparing the averages of improved processes with baseline estimates. In order to perform hypothesis testing, the population must be assumed constant and homogenous. Also, that samples are random and representative must be assumed.

Process

The first step in hypothesis testing is stating the null hypothesis, H_0. In most cases, the null hypothesis represents the value that the test aspires to prove. Since a hypothesis test only can reject the null hypothesis or fail to reject it, in some cases framing the null hypothesis as something to be disproved makes more sense. The next step in hypothesis testing is defining the alternative hypothesis (H_1). The alternative hypothesis should cover all of the area excluded from the null hypothesis. The third step is either setting a value for *p* or selecting a significance level (α). The significance level is the chance of incorrectly rejecting a true hypothesis in what is known as a Type 1 error. Generally, it is considered better to set a p value because this allows more freedom for adjustment later in the experiment. Next, samples are collected and statistics are calculated. The final step in hypothesis testing is drawing a conclusion.

Interpretation

Interpreting a hypothesis test is simple. If the calculated statistic is larger than the critical value of the test statistic for the given level of significance, then the null hypothesis must be rejected. If the critical value of the test statistic is larger, then the null hypothesis is not rejected. Software programs such as Excel or Minitab can use the calculated *p* value to indicate whether the obtained results are appropriate, assuming that the null hypothesis is true. If the p value is small, then the chances of obtaining results similar to those gathered during the experiment are so small that the null hypothesis should be rejected. If the null hypothesis is not rejected, the experiment is said to have reached a weak conclusion, because the means may or may not be equal. When the null hypothesis is confirmed, however, the experiment is said to have produced a strong conclusion, or a definitive statement that the means are not equal.

Nonparametric Tests on Equality of Means

For a nonparametric test on the equality of means, the null hypothesis H_0 will be that population 1's median is equal to population 2's median. The alternative hypothesis H_1, then, is that population 1's median does not equal population 2's median. Median is preferable to mean in these tests because it indicates central tendency regardless of distribution. The next step in the test involves declaring a significance level or *p* value. After samples have been collected, the probability of Type II error can be assessed. Upon completing the test, it is possible to compare the calculated statistics with a test statistic. The null hypothesis is rejected if the calculated statistic is greater than the critical value of the test statistic. If the calculated statistic does not exceed the critical value of the test statistic, then the null hypothesis cannot be rejected. Nonetheless, this rejection does not imply confirmation of the null hypothesis.

"5 Whys" Method of Problem-Solving

The "5 Whys" method is used to identify the underlying causes of a defect. The method is simple: the problem is stated, and the questioner asks why this problem exists. For example, if the problem is that workers always are late, the questioner will ask, "Why are the workers always late?" An answer is given, and this statement is then questioned. This pattern continues until the root cause is identified. A continuation of the above example might proceed as follows: "The workers always are late because parking takes a long time." "Why?" "Because there aren't enough parking spaces."

"Why?" "Because the company trucks are taking up multiple spaces in the lot...." And so on, until the root problem is identified and solved. More or less than five "whys" may be required to resolve the problem. This number was chosen as a guideline rather than a rule.

Criticisms

Some people criticize the "5 Whys" method of identifying underlying problems for being simplistic. One complaint about this method asserts that it encourages investigators to examine and resolve only the symptoms of a problem rather than addressing the true cause. Also, the "5 Whys" method does not require any further data-gathering, so it tends to be limited by the investigator's existing expertise. Furthermore, no part of the method encourages the investigator to consider a perspective other than his or her own. In addition, the "5 Whys" method tends to generate non-repeatable results, which cannot be duplicated or achieved by other investigators. One last criticism of the "5 Whys" method concerns its focus upon a single root cause while ignoring the possibility that a problem may have more than one cause.

Improve and Control Phases

Standardizing New Methods

The first task of the control stage is standardizing the new methods. The new protocols and processes should be in continuous improvement, but the advances made thus far should be written as policy. Too often, employees fall back into old and unproductive habits after the main thrust of the Six Sigma project is complete. One way to prevent this backsliding is to use process control to monitor process variation. One way to do this is to define the methods of control with a control plan. Another way involves writing out all process procedures and duties on process maps, flowcharts, and sets of work instructions. Process variation always should be monitored with process control. Finally, all employees should receive training in the new methods, and new employees should receive a comprehensive orientation.

Control Plans

A control plan is a general summary of the detection and/or prevention strategies used to control processes or materials. Control plans most often are used during the control stage of DMAIC. They are used to create a record of the strategy used to control the key process variables. A control plan generally is compiled from the results of designed experiments and failure modes and effects analysis. This latter analysis is important because it indicates the most important sources of failure to control. The characteristics that need to be monitored and controlled will be listed along the left side of the control chart. For each characteristic, there will be a specification, measurement technique, sample size, sample frequency, analytical tool, and reaction protocol.

Listed Information

A control plan typically provides six pieces of information for every characteristic: specification, measurement technique, sample size, sample frequency, analytical tool, and reaction protocol. The specification defines what is considered acceptable and unacceptable for this characteristic. It should be expressed as an objective value. For instance, the specification for an oven might be 400 degrees if it needs to be at this temperature in order to function properly. The measurement technique is the equipment and protocol for assessing the specifications. The sample size is the number of measurements required at every collection time. The sample frequency indicates the interval between each successive data collection. The analytical tool is the system for analyzing the measurements. For instance, some characteristics will be monitored with control charts, so any adverse trends can be detected. Finally, the reaction protocols on a control plan will be the directions for employees in the event that a characteristic requires adjustment.

Preventing Deviation

Statistical Process Control

In Six Sigma, it is preferable almost always to prevent mistakes then to correct mistakes that already have occurred. Detection after the mistake is more expensive, time-consuming, and difficult. Six Sigma teams find the inputs that lead to process variation. If the inputs are controlled, variations and errors can be minimized and even eliminated. Statistical process controls monitor the stability of input and output variables, although this process is more effective at monitoring inputs. If the process capability index C_{pk} is 1.5 or more, then a control chart may be used to assess the Six Sigma-level outputs are good enough. Statistical process control is one of the three common methods for controlling processes: the other two are engineering process control and operational procedures.

Engineering Process Control

Engineering process control (EPC) is a mechanical system for automatically adjusting input in reponse to process variations. A refrigerator is equipped with a basic engineering process control: when the temperature inside rises too far from the desired level, a cooling engine lowers the temperature. The engineering process control devices used in industry are much more complicated. They can function with multiple inputs and outputs. When engineering process control devices are used, however, one cannot also use statistical process control charts, because the constant adjustment of the EPC system will influence the data. In other words, when engineering process control devices are used, the data collected from the process is not independent.

Operational Procedures

Operational procedures are similar to engineering process control, except that humans, rather than machines, execute operational procedures. For this reason, operational procedures are subject to more errors. Still, in some cases, operational procedures still will be the best and cheapest option, especially in transactional processes. One common operational procedure is standardizing the process. For instance, the tellers at a bank could be taught to process deposits according to the same steps every time. Another operational procedure is separating orders by type. Many businesses streamline their responses to orders by dividing orders into several key categories. Another way to prevent deviation with operational procedures is establishing processes for diverting resources when needs are urgent. Operational procedures require careful observation and should be documented on process maps, flowcharts, or written summaries.

Basic Components of Control Plan

Control plans list all of the information related to error prevention and detection efforts. This information is based on designed experiments and failure modes and effects analysis. These processes indicate the processes and inputs that need to be monitored and controlled. The risk priority number generated during FMEA designates the most important failure modes in a process. A comprehensive control plan includes basic information such as the specification related to each relevant characteristic. On a control chart, the specification is the objective range within which the characteristic tolerably can fall. The control chart also should indicate how the characteristic will be measured and how many measurements will be included in each sample. A control chart also should indicate how often samples will be obtained and the analytical tool with which they will be evaluated. Finally, a complete control chart will include the reaction rules, the response protocols when the characteristic does not meet the specifications.

Statistical Process Control Charts

Statistical process control charts use past performance to predict future variations. These charts can confirm the stability of a process. Statistical process control charts are used during the measure, analyze, improve, and control stages of DMAIC. In the measure stage, they convert common-cause variation into objective data that can be used to baseline processes. Also, statistical control charts can be used during the measure stage to evaluate the repeatability and reproducibility of a measurement system. In the analyze stage, statistical control charts can be used to distinguish common and special causes of variation. In the improve stage, statistical control charts can be used to confirm the success of process improvements. Finally, in the control stage of DMAIC, statistical control charts can be used to confirm the stability of adjusted processes and to confirm that the adjustments have improved the process.

Creation

All control charts hold certain charactistics in common. First, the *x*-axis value must be sequential on every chart. Often, time is plotted along the *x*-axis. The *y*-axis, on the other hand, will be for the statistic being charted for each unit on the *x*-axis. Also, a statistical process control chart will define limits for the plotted statistic. Control limits are calculated by observing process behavior. In order for a control chart to work, it must be derived from rational sub-groups (samples), or short-term variation will not indicate long-term variation. A sub-group is considered rational if the causes of within-subgroup variation are approximately the same as the causes of between-subgroup variation. In other words, any observed variation should be random. Each subgroup will indicate the current location in the process and the amount of variation at that location.

Kaizen Philosophy

Kaizen is a Japanese philosophy that governs all aspects of business. In kaizen, constant efforts should improve the quality of the business. These improvements are continuous and subtle, unlike those produced by Western-style innovation. In kaizen, improvements are small and frequent. Many improvements are based on the insights and experiences of lower-level employees, in contrast to the Western business model, in which changes typically result from executive orders. The initial concern of the kaizen business is attracting and maintaining good employees. The kaizen philosophy asserts that good employees will make good processes inevitable. Kaizen can be successful only with adequate training, defined operating practices, and buy-in from all employees. Furthermore, in kaizen, constant communication exists between employees at all levels. Kaizen is one of the more effective systems of total quality management.

Flow, Pull, and Perfection

In the kaizen philosophy, flow is the quality of continuous process accomplishment. The goal of kaizen is to create continuous flow through the organization rather than improving limited areas of a process. When a process has good flow, materials and information do not wait between activities. Businesses tend to create inefficiencies when they focus only on flow in one or two areas. Instead, flow should be considered from the perspective of the entire business. Pull is another concept in kaizen. In this system, pull means that each activity in a process should receive only the necessary materials and resources when subsequent activities are demanding the process be completed. In other words, instead of pushing resources through the process chain, it is more effective to have them be drawn along by the vacancies created by completed projects down the line. Finally, in kaizen the term perfection is defined as the ultimate goal of continuous improvement. By eliminating waste and streamlining processes, an organization can approach perfection.

Kaizen Events

Kaizen is a Japanese system of continuous process improvement. The intention of a kaizen event is to implement quickly the continuous improvement strategy. This implementation usually takes between three and five days. The first step in a kaizen event is to train employees in the general principles of kaizen. The next step is to define the problem to be solved by this particular kaizen event and to frame the desired result in terms of a goal. Before progress can be made, the process as it currently exists must be measured. In some cases, the organization will realize during this stage that a sufficient measurement system never has been created for the process, in which case it may be necessary to devise one. This occurrence can extend the duration of the kaizen event. The next phase of a kaizen event is brainstorming, during which the participants generate possible solutions to the problem. All proposed solutions should indicate clearly the path from the present to the future state.

In the typical kaizen event, the next step after settling on a solution is implementation. As such, implementation can take a considerable amount of time, and results may not be definitive by the end of the event. However, the initial implementation may suggest some possible ways that the solution can be tweaked. Furthermore, a defined follow-up plan should define the method for making changes to the implemented process. After the solution has been implemented and a full cycle has passed, results should be gathered and presented to the rest of the company. The final stage of a kaizen event celebrating success. While this stage might sound trivial, it reinforces the value of the program and encourages similar projects in the future.

Lay-Offs

In order for kaizen to work, employees must be committed fully. However, this commitment can occur only when management has established a few fundamentals. First, the company must have a strict and explicit policy regarding lay-offs caused by kaizen projects. Employees never should worry that their improvement efforts will result in personal job loss. Of course, continuous improvements will reduce the need for employees in some areas of the business. These employees should not be laid off; instead, they should instead be transferred to a kaizen department where they can contribute to subsequent projects. In most cases, the implementation of kaizen will lead to greater demand in the future, so these transferred employees eventually will be required. Kaizen and other lean techniques always aim at increasing productivity by liberating resources. If demand does not increase, the organization can continue to improve until attrition brings the number of employees in line with needs.

Creating Effective Kaizen Culture

Managers must take specific steps to ensure that employees commit to continuous improvement. The first and most important of these steps is training every employee in the basics of kaizen. This training can be done during employee orientation or at the beginning of a kaizen event. Furthermore, managers must establish incentives for employee participation. Employees should be encouraged to make suggestions and contribute to the implementation of kaizen solutions. These incentives should be based on metrics related to employee performance rather than merely on results. In other words, employees should be rewarded based on their dedication to the kaizen program rather than the success of any particular improvement project. The incentives should be considered from the perspective of the employee. Finally, managers should give their employees chances to advance and accept more responsibility within the kaizen program. If employees view kaizen as a way to advance their own careers, they will be more likely to give it their best effort.

Basic Objectives of Improve Stage

The improve stage of DMAIC occurs when all of the hard work of the preceding sections finally is applied to processes. The first major objective of the improve stage is to set the new process operating conditions. These conditions are based on the experimentation and analysis of the measure and analyze phases. The next objective of the improve stage is to identify and address the failure modes for the new processes. Assessing and predicting the benefits of the proposed solution also is appropriate. Before making massive changes, the Six Sigma team should be able to guess how positive the results of these solutions will be. The final objective of the improve stage is to implement and confirm process improvements, the moment when the predictions developed during the preceding sections finally are tested against reality.

Redefining Process Flow

One way to improve processes is to redefine the process flows. A process may be simplified or optimized. Redundant steps may be removed, and level-loading techniques may be applied. Many businesses improve processes by reducing set-up times. Whenever process flows are redefined, assessing the impact on quality is important. The critical-to-quality metrics used during the measure stage are useful. Benchmarking is a common approach to redefining process flows. Benchmarking refers to a systematic review of similar or dissimilar processes in another organization. Too often, benchmarking is assumed a prelude to imitation. People incorrectly believe that benchmarking means mapping out a competitor's process and then copying it. Instead, businesses should use the information they obtain as inspiration.

Simulations

Many Six Sigma teams use simulations to inform their choices during the improve stage of DMAIC. A simulation is a cheap way to predict the likelihoods and effects of variable levels. Simulations can confirm the solutions derived from analysis and can indicate the possible interactions between variables. Simulations are useful for evaluating changing situations because the dynamics of the change can be built into the simulation. Simulations require a process model and a rough probability distribution for every variable. The simulation takes these distributions and creates a resulting frequency distribution. Simulations can be very informative, but they must be confirmed against hard data before or after they are run. Although simulations are not fool-proof method of research, they certainly are valuable relative to their cost.

Adjustment of Operating Conditions

During the improve stage, the Six Sigma team must identify or predict optimal operating conditions. This action can be difficult when many input factors contribute to performance. The overarching goal of adjusting operating conditions is to establish levels that provide satisfactory results with minimal variation. If the process model is complex, the best way to identify optimal operating conditions is with response surface techniques. These techniques narrow the regions in which optimal factor settings may occur. Another way to find the best operating conditions is with evolutionary operations, or EVOP. One advantage of EVOP is that it can be implemented as the process continues to run. Changes are made to the process in action instead of in an experimental condition.

Evaluation of Process Failure Modes

The initial goal during the improve stage of DMAIC is to optimize the process flow. Once this optimization is complete, the team will evaluate the new failure modes. In other words, the team will now examine the new operating conditions or process flows for possible sources of deviation. Once these conditions or flows are identified, the team will brainstorm possible solutions. These problems and potential solutions often are depicted on a process decision program chart, which looks a bit like a tree diagram. The process decision program chart is a good first step, but it usually must be supplemented by failure modes and effects analysis, or FMEA. A comprehensive FMEA concludes with the generation of a risk priority number (RPN), indicating the influence of a particular failure on overall performance. The team then must develop mitigation or elimination strategies for the most significant potential failures.

Quality Function Deployment

Quality function deployment, typically called by the initials QFD, is a system for ensuring that customer requirements are aligned with product and process requirements. Quality function deployment most often is used in the analyze and improve stages of DMAIC. In these stages, QFD is used to plot strategies for fulfilling customer requirements. The basic process of quality function deployment is to establish customer requirements, known as whats, and design requirements, known as hows. The customer requirements are what needs to be achieved, and the design requirements are how they will be achieved. A number of tables are used to assess the importance and significance of various design requirements in the promotion of customer requirements. If a customer requirement, or what, has very few or no design requirements, or hows, then improving the process may be possible. When there are hows without whats, the process may contain some non-value-added activities that can be eliminated.

X-Bar Charts

X-bar charts, sometimes called $\bar{X}$ charts, are control charts for variables data. These charts take the averages from subgroups (of observations) to get a view of the process location over time. X-bar charts are most useful during the measure, analyze, improve, and control stages of DMAIC. In the measure stage, they are used to baseline processes by identifying the inevitable amount of common-cause variation. They also are used in this stage to evaluate the repeatability and reproducibility of a measurement system. In the analyze stage, these charts are used to distinguish special and common causes of variation. In the improve stage, X-bar charts are used to confirm that implemented changes have improved the process metric. Finally, in the control stage, X-bar charts are used to ensure that processes remain statistically stable.

Implementation

X-bar charts are useful when subgroups of more than two observations can be measured. The *x*-axis of the X-bar chart is time, so the chart serves as a chronological model of the process, moving from left to right. Of course, all data entered into an X-bar chart must be assigned a time, or else special-cause variation may not be noticeable. If the size of the subgroup is greater than ten, then a range chart should not be used to monitor process variation, because it will do a poor job of estimating process sigma. Instead, a sigma chart should be used. If the subgroup sizes are 1, an exponentially weighted moving average or individual-X/moving-range chart may be used.

Required Calculations

A certain set of calculations are required for an X-bar chart. These charts can be generated by Excel and Minitab. Before an X-bar chart can be created, the team must determine the appropriate subgroup size and sampling frequency. The plotted statistic for an X-bar chart is the subgroup average. The centerline is the grand average. The upper control limits are calculated $\text{UCL}_{\bar{x}} = \bar{\bar{x}} + 3\left(\frac{\sigma_x}{\sqrt{n}}\right)$, and the lower control limits are calculated $\text{LCL}_{\bar{x}} = \bar{\bar{x}} - 3\left(\frac{\sigma_x}{\sqrt{n}}\right)$. In these equations, $\bar{\bar{x}}$ is the grand average and σ_x is process sigma. Process sigma is calculated with either the subgroup range or the subgroup sigma statistic.

Interpretation

Before interpreting the X-bar chart, one must first examine the range chart. When the range chart is out of control, the control limits on the X-bar chart will not be useful. When the range chart contains points outside of statistical control, the special causes of this variation must be identified and eliminated. Some range charts will have only a few distinct values, suggesting that the chart needs better resolution. After any points outside statistical control have been removed, the X-bar chart may be interpreted relative to control limits and run-test rules. Any points on the X-bar chart outside statistical control must be eliminated. This elimination is accomplished in the usual way: the special causes of variation are identified through brainstorming and data analysis, and the operating conditions are adjusted accordingly.

Range and Sigma Charts

The plotted statistic for a range chart is calculated as follows: $\text{Range}_j = \max(x_1, x_2, \dots, x_n) - \min(x_1, x_2, \dots, x_n)$. The centerline is the average range. The upper control limits are calculated $\text{UCL}_R = \bar{R} + 3d_3\sigma_x$ and the lower control limits are calculated $\text{LCL}_R = \max(0, \bar{R} - 3d_3\sigma_x)$. In these equations, $\bar{R}$ is the average range, d_3 is a function of *n*, and σ_x is process sigma. In the calculation of process sigma, the average range is set as $\bar{R}/d_2$. In a sigma chart, the plotted statistic is the subgroup standard deviation, calculated $S_j = \sqrt{\frac{\sum_{i=1}^{n}(x_i - \bar{x}_j)^2}{n-1}}$, where x_i are the observations in subgroup j, $\bar{x}_j$ is the subgroup average for subgroup j, and n is the subgroup size. The centerline of the sigma chart is the average sigma. The upper control limits are calculated $\mathrm{UCL}_s = \bar{S} + 3\left(\frac{\bar{S}}{c_4}\right)\sqrt{1-c_4^2}$, and the lower control limits are calculated $\mathrm{LCL}_s = \min\left[0, \bar{S} + 3(\bar{S}/c_4)\sqrt{1-c_4^2}\right]$, where $\bar{S}$ is the average sigma and c_4 is a function of n.

PERT Analysis

Program evaluation and review techniques (PERT) analysis is used to estimate the time required by various processes. Furthermore, PERT is an essential part of scheduling and cycle time analysis in which hard data on the duration of certain process steps may be unobtainable. PERT analysis uses probability techniques to determine a best guess about durations. PERT analysis is used during the define, analyze, and improve stages of DMAIC. In the define stage, PERT analysis is used to identify the steps in a process with the most influence on the overall duration of the process. In the analyze stage, PERT analysis is used to determine the critical path of a process cycle. During the improve stage, PERT analysis is used to confirm improvements in the cycle time.

FMEA

Failure modes and effects analysis (FMEA) is a system for identifying extremely risky processes or features. The main criteria for this identification are that either the failure of the process will be very damaging or that a failure could occur unnoticed. Failure modes and effects analysis is primarily useful during the analyze, improve, and design stages of DMAIC. In the analyze stage, failure modes and effects analysis is used to identify and rank risky processes or product features. In the improve and design stages, failure modes and effects analysis is used to identify potentially risky activities or features in a planned improvement. A failure modes and effects analysis produces a risk priority number, which quantifies the severity, likelihood, and possibility for remediation of various accidents.

Creation

The creation of a failure modes and effects analysis (FMEA) begins with the identification of each step in a process or each feature in a product design. The next move is to identify all of the possible errors and mistakes for each step or feature. This list should be comprehensive, so it may take some time to create. The list also should indicate the results of each possible failure or error. In the next phase of FMEA, the severity of each possible failure or error should be ratedA number of standardized tables exist for ranking failure/error severity. Of course, it is impossible to rate the severity of failures in an objective manner. The next phase of FMEA is to gauge the likelihood of the failure or error. Again, this assessment typically is placed on a scale from one to ten. Next, the FMEA will focus on detection. The team should make a list of the mode of detection as well as the likelihood that failure will be detected (again, placed on a scale from one to ten). Finally, the ratings of severity, likelihood, and detection level are multiplied to produce a risk priority number (RPN). Possible failures are then ranked in order of descending RPN.

Interpretation

If severity, likelihood, and detection level each are rated on a ten-point scale, then the highest possible risk priority number will be 1000. The larger the number, the greater the risk. The interpretation and use of failure modes and effects analysis varies by organization. Some businesses establish a particular benchmark RPN and investigate any failures that score above it. One benefit of FMEA is its indication whether the severity, likelihood, or detection level of a failure needs attention. When severity must be reduced, redesigning the product or process entirely typically is necessary. Reducing the likelihood of the failure often is the most cost-effective solution and therefore is a primary target of Six Sigma efforts. Reducing the detection level can be effective, but it does not improve the product or process in any way.

5S

5S is a lean tool whose name is derived from a set of Japanese words related to organizational hygiene: organization, purity, cleanliness, discipline, and tidiness. For the purposes of American audiences, these words are sometimes translated as sort, straighten, shine, standardize, and sustain. 5S is used most often during the improve stage of DMAIC. Here, it is a valuable strategy for reducing cycle time that does not add value and that is lost to movement, finding lost materials, and inefficiently using the physical space. 5S may also be used to accelerate inventory processes and to diminish accidents in the workplace. The program is implemented according to a five-level system. At the first level, the organization has not been subjected to lean management processes. By the time the fifth level is reached, maximum efficiency and minimum waste have been achieved. In Six Sigma, the data collected according to such a rating system often is placed on a radar chart, which indicates the strengths and weaknesses of each department.

Cost-Benefit Analysis

Cost-benefit analysis is a rigorous evaluation of the consequences of a business decision. It attempts to simply decision-making by weighing the possible positive consequences of a decision with the burdens created by it. Businesses perform cost-benefit analysis before purchasing equipment, introducing new products, or hiring new employees. A comprehensive cost-benefit analysis will include not only the immediate consequences but also the second- and third-level consequences of a decision. A full cost-benefit analysis has three components: a preliminary survey, a feasibility study, and a final report. In the preliminary survey, the team gathers information about the decision. The feasibility study estimates the degree to which the idea will fulfill the requirements of customers. Finally, the final report presents the team's findings. The cost-benefit analysis may be stopped at any point if it is determined that the negative consequences outweigh the positive.

Six Sigma Practice Test

1. In businesses that apply the theory of constraints, which element of a process receives immediate attention?

a. The most problematic
b. The most important
c. The most efficient
d. The most complicated

2. What is one major problem with obtaining information about customer satisfaction from comment cards?

a. Participants must be compensated.
b. The most pleased and displeased customers are overrepresented.
c. Responses are often vague.
d. The expense is high.

3. Which distribution is appropriate for a continuous set of data with a fixed lower boundary but no upper boundary?

a. Johnson
b. exponential
c. normal
d. Lognormal

4. What are the three most important characteristics of process metrics?

a. Rationality, reliability, and repeatability
b. Reliability, reproducibility, and repeatability
c. Reliability, responsibility, and rationality
d. Repeatability, responsibility, and reproducibility

5. Which pioneer of quality control wrote *Quality Is Free*?

a. W. Edward Deming
b. Joseph M. Juran
c. Armand V. Feigenbaum
d. Philip B. Crosby

6. Which of the following conflict-response strategies would be most appropriate when a group is fragile?

a. Collaboration
b. Competition
c. Avoidance
d. Accommodation

7. Which key performance indicator is calculated by subtracting current costs from ideal costs?

a. Cost of poor quality
b. Revenue growth
c. Competitive quality
d. Performance on quality improvement

8. How is takt time calculated?

a. Available time divided by demand
b. Overall process time minus time required for a particular task
c. Demand divided by the amount of time available
d. Time required for a task divided by demand

9. How many runs would be required in a complete factorial design if there are four levels and three factors?

a. 7
b. 12
c. 64
d. 81

10. Which parameter of a statistical distribution relates to the weight of the tails relative to the center of the distribution?

a. Central tendency
b. Kurtosis
c. Skewness
d. Standard deviation

11. What is the name for the amount of completed product divided by the original amount of product?

a. Scrap rate
b. Throughput yield
c. Yield
d. Rolled throughput yield

12. Which method of creating a prioritization matrix is appropriate when time is limited?

a. Partial analytical method
b. Consensus-criteria method
c. Full analytical method
d. Summary method

13. In gauge repeatability and reproducibility analysis, what percentage of total process variation is acceptable?

a. 10% or less
b. 15% or less
c. 20% or less
d. 30% or less

14. Which type of diagram is used to eliminate unnecessary movement during a process?

a. Spaghetti diagram
b. Scatter diagram
c. Ishikawa diagram
d. Matrix diagram

15. In what stage of DMAIC would one expect to use a process decision program chart?

a. Improve
b. Define
c. Measure
d. Control

16. During which phase of response surface analysis is the direction of maximum response identified using the steepest ascent methodology?

a. Phase 0
b. Phase 1
c. Phase 2
d. Phase 3

17. In which method of sampling is a population divided into groups and a sample taken from each group?

a. Systematic sampling
b. Stratified sampling
c. Judgment sampling
d. Cluster sampling

18. In an analysis of variance, how is the F statistic used?

a. To compare the mean square treatment with the mean square error
b. To estimate the process average
c. To find the variation within each subgroup
d. To find the variation between different subgroups

19. Which of the following characteristics of a team most often results in groupthink?

a. Frequent communication
b. Lack of accountability
c. Lack of subject expertise
d. Undefined roles

20. In response surface analysis, which of the following values for *s* and *t* weights would indicate that the target value and the boundaries are equally important?

a. -3
b. 0
c. 1
d. 0.7

21. Which of the following would be considered a value-added activity?

a. Design
b. Delivery
c. Marketing
d. Manufacturing

22. Which type of human error is typically limited to a particular task?

a. Willful
b. Inadvertent
c. Technique
d. Selective

23. Which of the following is a disadvantage of using engineering process control devices to prevent deviation?

a. The devices must be monitored by human operators.
b. The use of these devices precludes the use of statistical process controls.
c. These devices require constant maintenance.
d. These devices cannot handle multiple inputs.

24. Which type of chart is appropriate when sample size is variable and each sample may contain more than one instance of the targeted condition?

a. P chart
b. Autocorrelation chart
c. U chart
d. X-bar chart

25. From whose perspective is value defined in the lean methodology?

a. Customer
b. Chief executive
c. Entry-level employee
d. Competitor

26. On an X-bar chart, what variable is always represented on the *x*-axis?

a. Variations
b. Errors
c. Length
d. Time

27. Which of the following diagrams indicates the critical path of a process?

a. Gantt chart
b. Work breakdown structure
c. Value stream analysis
d. Matrix diagram

28. Which of the following is a disadvantage of higher-order multiple regression models?

a. These models do a poor job of defining the area around a stationary point.
b. Comprehensive and detailed experiments must be performed on the main effects.
c. These models rarely have clear peaks and valleys.
d. Small regions are difficult to perceive.

29. If there are 32 observations in an experiment, it is typical to run autocorrelations from lag 1 to:

a. Lag 4
b. Lag 8
c. Lag 16
d. Lag 32

30. During which stage of DMAIC is it most useful to calculate process velocity?

a. Analyze
b. Define
c. Control
d. Improve

31. In kaizen, the idea that one step in a process should be completed only when the subsequent steps are ready is referred to as:

a. Flow
b. Poka-yoke
c. Pull
d. Perfection

32. Which type of Pareto chart would be the least useful?

a. One in which the bars represent costs
b. One in which the cumulative percentage line is steep
c. One in which all the bars are roughly the same height
d. One in which the bars on the left are significantly taller than the bars on the right

33. If all of the data points on an *Np* chart fall between the upper and lower control limits, the process is:

a. Representative
b. Stable
c. Efficient
d. Erratic

34. According to Little's law, the number of items included in a process divided by the number of process completions per hour is the:

a. Process lead time
b. Value-added time
c. Velocity
d. Process cycle efficiency

35. In nominal group technique, how many pieces of paper should each participant receive if there are 40 options to be considered?

a. 2
b. 4
c. 6
d. 8

36. When a batch sample has upper and lower specifications, which statistic is used in the creation of a process performance index?

a. P_p
b. P_{pk}
c. P_{pl}
d. C_p

37. Which of the following factors is not included in the calculation of risk priority number?

a. Detection level
b. Severity
c. Expense
d. Likelihood

38. Which of the following run tests identifies shifts in the process mean?

a. Run test 4
b. Run test 6
c. Run test 7
d. Run test 8

39. Which of the following autocorrelation functions would indicate the strongest correlation?

a. 0.1
b. -0.8
c. 0.9
d. -0.2

40. Which distribution should be used when the targeted characteristic may appear more than once per unit?

a. Binomial
b. Exponential
c. Lognormal
d. Poisson

41. Which Six Sigma methodology is more appropriate for existing processes?

a. DMADV
b. IDOV
c. DMAIC
d. DFSS

42. Which of the following distributions would be appropriate for discrete data?

a. Exponential
b. Poisson
c. Normal
d. Johnson

43. Which goodness-of-fit test focuses on the relationship between number of data points and distributional fit?

a. Nonparametric test
b. Kolmogorov-Smirnov test
c. Chi-square test
d. Anderson-Darling test

44. In hypothesis testing, why is it better to set a *p* value than to select a significance level?

a. It ensures that a true hypothesis will not be rejected.
b. It is then easier to make adjustments later in the experiment.
c. It enables the collection of more samples.
d. It makes it possible to reject the null hypothesis.

45. How are decisions represented in the ANSI set of flowchart symbols?

a. Circles
b. Squares
c. Rectangles
d. Diamonds

46. During which stage of DMAIC is the 5S method used most often?

a. Define
b. Measure
c. Analyze
d. Improve

47. In a histogram, the number of bars is equal to:

a. The square root of the total number of data values
b. The square root of the range of data
c. The range of data divided by the total number of data values
d. The number of data observations

48. Which statistical distribution is appropriate for continuous data with neither an upper nor a lower boundary?

a. Lognormal
b. Weibull
c. Exponential
d. Normal

49. In a contour plot, what is indicated by a series of evenly spaced parallel lines?

a. First-order main effects
b. Second-order main effects
c. Interactions between two responses
d. Interactions between three responses

50. Which of the following increases the power of an estimation of the confidence interval on the mean?

a. A sample population with a normal distribution
b. A smaller number of samples
c. A known standard deviation
d. An unknown standard deviation

Answer Key and Explanations

1. A: The most problematic. In businesses that apply the theory of constraints, the most problematic element of a process receives immediate attention. Indeed, the most problematic area is known as the constraint. The focus of improvement will be reducing the constraint without diminishing performance in any other area of the process. Once the targeted constraint has been diminished so that is no longer the most problematic component of the process, another area of the process will be addressed.

2. B: The most pleased and displeased customers are overrepresented. One major problem with obtaining information about customer satisfaction from comment cards is that the most pleased and displeased customers are overrepresented. That is, customers who have extreme opinions, whether positive or negative, will be the most motivated to comment. Businesses that use comment cards may find them to be a valuable source of specific information, but should avoid assuming that commenters are representative of the larger body of customers. Some of the advantages of comment cards are that they are relatively inexpensive and tend to elicit detailed feedback. Also, participation by customers is voluntary and does not require compensation.

3. D: Lognormal. A lognormal distribution is appropriate for a continuous set of data with a fixed lower boundary but no upper boundary. In most cases, the lower boundary on a lognormal distribution is zero. These distributions can be tested with a goodness-of-fit test. A Johnson distribution is more appropriate for continuous data that for whatever reason is inappropriate for a normal or exponential distribution. An exponential distribution is appropriate for any set of continuous data, though these distributions are most often used for frequency data. A normal distribution is appropriate for a set of continuous data with neither an upper nor a lower boundary. The normal distribution follows the pattern of the classic bell curve.

4. B: Reliability, reproducibility, and repeatability. The three most important characteristics of process metrics are reliability, reproducibility, and repeatability. Reliability is the extent to which the results of an experiment can be trusted to represent accurately the process being measured. Reproducibility is the extent to which a metric can be applied in different situations and obtain a reliable result. Repeatability is the extent to which a metric can be applied to the same situation multiple times and achieve the same result.

5. D: Philip B. Crosby. Philip B. Crosby wrote *Quality is Free*, a book that revolutionized quality management by placing an explicit emphasis on getting processes right the first time. Crosby insisted that businesses are better served by investing more money in quality control on the first run, and thereby avoiding the costs of defective products. W. Edwards Deming is famous for enumerating the seven deadly diseases of the workplace and fourteen points of emphasis for management. Joseph M. Juran stressed the importance of customer satisfaction as a goal of quality control. Armand V. Feigenbaum is known for emphasizing four key actions in the implementation of quality management: establishing standards; creating metrics for conformance to these standards; resolving issues that impede conformance; and planning for continuous improvement.

6. D: Accommodation. When a group is fragile, the most appropriate conflict response strategy would be accommodation. Accommodation is the temporary sacrifice of personal desires in the name of group consensus. If a group is in danger of falling apart, the best way to handle a conflict may be to temporarily put aside differences in order to make progress in other areas. Collaboration or competition may be too risky for a fragile group, and avoidance of the conflict only jeopardizes the long-term health of the group by failing to resolve the underlying issues.

7. A: Cost of poor quality. The *cost of poor quality* is calculated by subtracting current costs from ideal costs. This is just a rough estimate as the exact value of the cost of poor quality is unknowable. The point of estimating the cost of poor quality is to get a general idea of what savings could be made available through remediation and improvement efforts. *Revenue growth* is calculated by determining the net increase in sales figures over a particular interval. *Competitive quality* is an umbrella term for a set of metrics related to the parts of performance that have the most influence on sales. Some competitive quality measures depend on obtaining information from customers. *Performance on quality improvement,* finally, is a subjective metric that includes the number of completed and active projects, the financial results of these projects, and the number of employees and hours required for the project.

8. A: Time available divided by the demand. Takt time is calculated by dividing the amount of time available by the demand. This value, which is also known as target process time, should be posted at each workstation during the process of level loading. The takt time is the maximum amount of time a process can take without slowing down the overall completion of the task.

9. C: 64. If there are four levels and three factors in a complete factorial design, 64 runs would be required. The number of required runs is calculated by raising the number of levels to a power equal to the number of factors. In this case, then, the calculation is performed $4^3 = 64$. If the complete factorial design had five levels and three factors, the number of runs would be calculated $5^3 = 125$.

10. B: Kurtosis. Kurtosis is the parameter that measures the "tailedness" of a distribution or the propensity to produce outliers. In a normal distribution, the kurtosis value is 3. If the tails contain more of the probability mass (more extreme values), the kurtosis value will be higher than 3; if the tails are less extreme, the kurtosis value will be less than 3. Despite common misconceptions, kurtosis does not measure peak sharpness. Central tendency is the general trend of the data: in an asymmetrical distribution, the median is roughly equivalent to the central tendency, while in an asymmetrical distribution, the mean is a better marker. Skewness is basically the difference between the mean and the mode of a data set. The mode of the data set is the value that appears most often. Finally, the standard deviation of the data set is the average amount of variation from the mean.

11. C: Yield. Yield is the amount of completed product divided by the original amount of product. This is one of the more popular critical-to-quality metrics. The ideal yield is one (or 100%). Scrap rate, meanwhile, is the percentage of materials not ultimately used in products. Throughput yield is the average percentage of completed units with no defects. Rolled throughput yield, finally, is the quality level that can be anticipated after several steps in the process have been completed.

12. B: Consensus-criteria method. When time is limited, the consensus-criteria method should be used to create a prioritization matrix. In this method, a group of people is each allotted a hundred points, which they then allocate across a series of criteria according to perceived importance. Prioritization matrices are used to identify those projects that will create the most value improvement over the long term. Also, organizations use participation matrices to identify the projects that will contribute the most to the achievement of the organizational goals. Besides the consensus-criteria method, the other method for creating a prioritization matrix is called the full analytical method. In this method, all of the various options are listed, and the members of the team assign a numerical value to each.

13. A: 10% or less. In gauge repeatability and reproducibility analysis, 10% or less total process variation is acceptable. Variation from 10 to 30% is considered problematic, and any variation over 30% is unacceptable. A gauge repeatability and reproducibility analysis may result in a statistic expressed as a percentage of total process variation or a percentage of tolerance. The range of acceptable percentages is the same when the statistic generated is a percentage of tolerance. Gauge repeatability and reproducibility analysis indicates the degree to which a measurement system avoids common- and special-cause variation.

14. A: Spaghetti diagram. A spaghetti diagram indicates the physical travel of employees, resources, and equipment during a process. These diagrams are used to identify unnecessary movements and to streamline processes as much as possible. A scatter diagram displays the correlation between two variables, with the independent variable on the *x*-axis and the dependent variable on the *y*-axis. An Ishikawa diagram, also known as a fishbone or cause-and-effect diagram, is used to outline the causes of a particular event, as well as the possible results of particular actions. Finally, a matrix diagram depicts the relationships between a group of different items in several groups. A matrix diagram looks a great deal like a table of data, with the strength between relationships indicated by the values in each cell.

15. A: Improve. A process decision program chart is used to isolate possible problems with a particular process or strategy. These charts are typically used during the Analyze and Improve stages of DMAIC. At the top of the chart, the process is named. The steps in the process are usually presented chronologically, with any necessary substeps mentioned underneath. Then the potential problems in each step are listed, along with some brainstormed solutions.

16. B: Phase 1. During Phase 1 of response surface analysis, the direction of maximum response is identified with the steepest ascent methodology. This methodology is also used to define the current operating region. Phase 0 involves the use of screening designs to assemble a basic list of significant factors and create a first-order regression model. Phase 2 is the application of ridge analysis and a second-order model. The intention of Phase 2 of response surface analysis is to identify optimal conditions at the stationary points in a limited region. There is no Phase 3 in response surface analysis.

17. B: Stratified sampling. In stratified sampling, the population is divided into groups, and a sample is taken from each group. In systematic sampling, on the other hand, there is a particular order to the selection of samples. In judgment sampling, an expert or group of experts selects the samples. In cluster sampling, experts create a representative group from which a random sample is drawn.

18. A: To compare the mean square treatment with the mean square error. In an analysis of variance, the F statistic is used to compare the mean square treatment with the mean square error. The mean square treatment is the average variation between the subsets, while the mean square error is the sum of the squares of the residuals. In order to trust the results of the F statistic, one must assume that the subsets have a normal distribution and unequal variance. The variation within each subgroup is calculated by taking repeated samples from the subgroup. The variation between different subgroups is found by comparing the averages of each subgroup.

19. C: Lack of subject expertise. When a team has a lack of subject expertise, it is more likely to suffer from groupthink. Groupthink is a phenomenon in which team members agree too readily, without adequately challenging each other's ideas. When groupthink occurs, a team will often select the first proposed solution to a problem, even if it has serious weaknesses. Groupthink is more likely to be a problem when the team members do not have enough experience or expertise in the subject area to come up with alternatives to a recommendation. Also, if the team members do not feel empowered to offer their views, they may be more likely to engage in groupthink.

20. B: 0. In phase 2 of response surface analysis, the *s* and *t* weights are based on the relationship between the target and the boundary. When the target and the boundary have equal value, the *s* and *t* weights are 0. When the target is more important than the boundary, the *t* weight is between 0.1 and 1.

21. D: Manufacturing. Manufacturing is considered a value-added activity. Value-added activities are those that create value in a product or service from the perspective of the customer. There are certain processes that are necessary but that do not add value for the customer. These are known as business-value-added activities. Design, delivery, and marketing are classic examples of business-value-added activities, because they do not directly add value for the customer, but they are a necessary part of the production process.

22. C: Technique. Technique error is typically limited to a particular task. Six Sigma experts identify three categories of human error: technique, inadvertent, and willful. Technique errors are the result of a lack of comprehension or poor training. It is more likely that technique errors will occur on difficult tasks. Inadvertent errors are slightly different, because they occur by accident even when an employee is experienced and understands the task. It is impossible to eliminate entirely inadvertent errors so long as there are human operators. A willful error is made intentionally by an employee. The best way to reduce willful errors is to maintain high morale and incentivize high performance.

23. B: The use of these devices precludes the use of statistical process controls. One disadvantage of using engineering process controls to prevent deviation is that the use of these devices precludes the use of statistical process controls. An engineering process control is a mechanism that automatically adjusts inputs when it detects variations in the process. A thermostat is a basic example of an engineering process control. It is not necessary for these devices to be monitored by human operators, and in most cases engineering process controls do not require constant maintenance. The constant adjustments made by these devices, however, mean that any data related to their activities is not independent, and therefore cannot be analyzed with statistical process control charts. However, the engineering process controls used by heavy industry are capable of handling a number of different inputs and outputs simultaneously.

24. C: U chart. A U chart is appropriate when sample size is variable and each sample may contain more than one instance of the targeted condition. These are control charts most appropriate for handling attributes data. A P chart, on the other hand, is better for measuring the percentage of samples with a particular characteristic when sample size is variable and the characteristic will either be present or absent. An autocorrelation chart indicates the relationships between various factors in the process. An X-bar chart, finally, is a control chart for variables data, in which the subgroup averages are assessed to determine the process location variation over time.

25. A: Customer. In the lean methodology, value is always defined from the perspective of the customer. This was a radical shift in perspective when it was first introduced. Most businesses assessed value from the perspective of executives or in-house experts. In lean methodology, value is defined as the qualities or characteristics for which a customer is willing to compensate the business.

26. D: Time. On an X-bar chart, time is always represented on the *x*-axis. X-bar charts are control charts for variables data. The chart should resemble a chronological model of the process: as the bars move away from the y-axis, they represent the advancement of time. In order for an X-bar chart to be possible, any variation must be assigned a time value. Outlying values on the X-bar chart indicate the presence of special-cause variation.

27. A: Gantt chart. A Gantt chart indicates the critical path of a process. The critical path is the sequence of steps that have a direct bearing on the overall length of the process. Some steps can be delayed without elongating the overall duration of the process: these steps are not considered to be on the critical path. A work breakdown structure depicts the organization of a process. To create a work breakdown structure, one isolates the various components of a problem and then considers the various contingencies associated with each component. A value stream analysis determines the elements of a process that add value to the finished product. These elements are targeted for special attention. Finally, a matrix diagram depicts the relative strengths of the relationships between the items in different groups. A matrix diagram might indicate causal relationships between various factors in a process or might simply indicate which of the factors are related.

28. B: Comprehensive and detailed experiments must be performed on the main effects. One disadvantage of higher-order multiple regression models is that comprehensive and detailed experiments must be performed on the main effects. Otherwise, it will not be wise to assume that the results of the higher-order multiple regression models are useful or accurate. However, higher-order multiple regression models have a number of advantages. For one thing, they are excellent at clearly defining the area around a stationary point. They typically have well-defined peaks and valleys, which facilitates analysis. Also, they are very effective at mapping small regions in the process, so they are able to achieve a high level of precision and detail.

29. B: Lag 8. If there are 32 observations in an experiment, it is typical to run autocorrelations from lag 1 to lag 8. The basic calculation for the number of autocorrelations in an experiment is lag 1 to lag $x/4$, in which x is the number of observations. Since there are 32 observations in this experiment, autocorrelations should run from lag 1 to lag 8. The lag is the difference between correlated observations. In lag 1, for instance, observation 1 is correlated with observation 2, observation 2 is correlated with observation 3, and observation 3 is correlated with observation 4, and so on. In lag 8, observation 1 would be correlated with observation 9, observation 2 with observation 10, observation 3 with observation 11, and so on. An experiment with 32 observations would include all of the intervening correlations between lag 1 and lag 8 (that is, lags 2 through 7).

30. A: Analyze. It is most useful to calculate process velocity during the analyze stage of DMAIC. Process velocity is the rate at which a particular phase of the process adds value. Obviously, the higher the process velocity, the better. This metric is most useful during the analyze stage of DMAIC because it can be used to prioritize methods for improving cycle time. Velocity is typically calculated by dividing the number of value-added steps by the process lead time, which is the number of items in the process divided by the number of process completions per hour. Of course, as with any metric of quality, process velocity is somewhat subjective.

31. C: Pull. In kaizen, the idea that one step in a process should be completed only when the subsequent steps are ready is referred to as pull. This is opposite to the typical arrangement in manufacturing processes, in which materials are pushed through the process chain as they are completed. Kaizen recommends instead that materials be drawn along by vacuums created in the production chain. A process chain in which this occurs is said to have pull. Flow, meanwhile, is the continuous completion of a process. Organizations that adopt the kaizen philosophy attempt to make flow constant in every department and stage of processes. Poka-yoke is a Japanese system for error-proofing, based on the premise that avoiding errors in the first run is worth a slightly higher cost. Perfection is the kaizen ideal of continuous improvement. Perfection is a goal that can never be attained but should be strived towards regardless.

32. C: One in which all the bars are roughly the same height. The least useful type of Pareto chart would be one in which all the bars are roughly the same height. A Pareto chart is used to identify the most important and urgent problems in a process. It is based on the Pareto principle, which is basically that a process can be improved dramatically through attention to the few most important problems. It is essential that the bars on a Pareto chart represent fungible values, like cost or count. A Pareto chart will not be useful if it is based on percentages or rates. The most useful Pareto charts have several large bars on the left, indicating problems that are significantly more important than others. Similarly, a steeply ascending line on a Pareto chart indicates that a few of the identified factors are very important, and therefore that the chart will be useful. If all of the bars on a Pareto chart are roughly the same height, no one factor is more important than another, meaning it will be impossible to generate an unusual amount of benefit by solving a single problem.

33. B: Stable. If all of the data points on an *Np* chart fall between the upper and lower control limits, the process is stable. So long as all of the variation is within these limits, it can be assumed to be the result of common causes. Assuming the chart is reliable, data points that fall outside the upper and lower control limits are the result of special-cause variation. At the least, the presence of data points outside the upper and lower control limits identifies areas where employees will need to conduct further research. *Np* charts are control charts for analyzing attributes data. These charts are used when the sample size is regular and the targeted condition may only occur once per sample.

34. A: Process lead time. According to Little's law, the number of items included in a process divided by the number of process completions per hour is the process lead time. Process cycle efficiency is calculated by dividing value-added time by process lead time. When every activity in the process adds value, the process may attain the maximum process cycle efficiency of 100%. Of course, very few processes actually reach this level of efficiency. It is much more common for a process to have a process cycle efficiency below 50%.

35. D: 8. In nominal group technique, each participant should receive eight pieces of paper if there are 40 options to be considered. Each participant will then write one of the options down on each piece of paper, along with its rank (first through eighth). It is typical for each participant to receive eight pieces of paper when there are more than 35 options. When there are from 20 to 35 options, the typical number of papers for each person is six. When there are fewer than 20 options to be considered, it is typical for each member of the group to receive four pieces of paper. Once all of the group members turn in their rankings, the various options are compared, and the most popular are given further consideration.

36. A: P_p. When a batch sample has upper and lower specifications, the P_p statistic is used in the creation of a process performance index. If the batch sample has either an upper or a lower specification but not both, the P_{pk} statistic may be used. If the distributions are not normal, the C_p statistic is used to calculate the process performance indices.

37. C: Expense. Expense is not one of the factors included in the calculation of risk priority number. Risk priority number is calculated by multiplying severity, likelihood, and detection level. The severity of the risk is the significance of its occurrence. Various industries have created standardized tables for indicating the severity of common risks. The likelihood of a risk is simply the chances of it happening. Finally, the detection level is based on the number of modes for identifying the error or failure, as well as the chances that any one of these modes will be successful in detection. A common formula for calculating risk priority number is to place all of these categories on a scale from 1 to 10, then multiply them together. In this scenario, the maximum risk priority number would be 1,000.

38. B: Run test 6. Run test 6 identifies shifts in the process mean. The other run tests provide information about sampling errors. Run tests 1, 2, 3, and 5 also identify shifts in the process mean. Run tests are typically used in statistical process control programs to identify errors in data collection. Unfortunately, run tests are only able to identify the *presence* of errors and are not very good at pinpointing their location.

39. C: 0.9. An autocorrelation function of 0.9 would indicate the strongest correlation. The range of autocorrelation functions and partial autocorrelation functions extends from -1 to 1. The strength of the correlation is indicated by the distance from zero (that is, the absolute value), regardless of whether the value is on the positive or negative side. Therefore, an autocorrelation function of 0.9 would indicate a stronger correlation than would functions of 0.1, -0.8, and -0.2.

40. D: Poisson. A Poisson distribution should be used when the targeted characteristic may appear more than once per unit. In order for a Poisson distribution to be effective, the data should consist of positive whole numbers and the experimental trials should be independent. A binomial distribution is appropriate for situations in which the units in the population will only have one of two possible characteristics (for example, off or on). An exponential distribution is appropriate for measurement data, especially frequency. A lognormal distribution is appropriate for continuous data with a fixed lower boundary but no upper boundary. In most cases, the lower boundary of a lognormal distribution is zero.

41. C: DMAIC. The Six Sigma methodology of DMAIC (define, measure, analyze, improve, and control) is most appropriate for handling existing processes. It is geared toward gradual improvement. DMADV (define, measure, analyze, design, and verify), on the other hand, includes a design phase, during which new products can be developed. On occasion, DMADV is used to give existing products a large-scale remodeling. IDOV (identification, design, optimization, and validation) is the primary methodology of DFSS (design for Six Sigma). The main difference between DFSS and DMAIC is that the former attempts to prevent rather than reduce defects.

42. B: Poisson. A Poisson distribution would be most appropriate for discrete data. Binomial distributions may also be used for discrete data. Continuous data, on the other hand, should be handled with a normal, exponential, Johnson, or Pearson distribution. Continuous data is obtained from measurement, while discrete data is based on observation. A discrete data set, for instance, would only indicate the number of times an event occurred, but would not give any indication of the size or intensity of the event.

43. B: Kolmogorov-Smirnov test. The Kolmogorov-Smirnov test focuses on the relationship between number of data points and distributional fit. A nonparametric test is used instead of a hypothesis test for comparing the means from samples with different conditions and for assessing the effects of changes on process averages. A chi-square test is the simplest form of goodness-of-fit test. An Anderson-Darling test is excellent for obtaining information from the extreme ends of a distribution.

44. B: It is then easier to make adjustments later in the experiment. In hypothesis testing, it's better to set a *p* value than to select a significance level because it is then easier to make adjustments later in the experiment. In general, a *p* value allows for more freedom in the later parts of the experiment. There is always a possibility of rejecting a true hypothesis, in what is known as a

Type 1 error. The number of samples collected is not dependent on whether a *p* value is set or a significance level is selected, and either method maintains the possibility that the null hypothesis will be rejected.

45. D: Diamonds. In the ANSI (American National Standards Institute) set of flowchart symbols, decisions are represented with diamonds. There are other symbols to represent different types of tasks, but many simple flowcharts will simply use the diamond for decisions and rectangles for all other tasks in the process. An excessive number of decisions on a flowchart is a common symptom of inefficiency.

46. D: Improve. The 5S method is used most often during the improve stage of DMAIC. 5S is a Japanese lean tool for reducing cycle time. In Japanese, the five aspects of 5S are organization, purity, cleanliness, discipline, and tidiness. In English, these words are often translated as sort, straighten, shine, standardize, and sustain. The most common targets of 5S programs are processes that tend to lose materials or require unnecessary movement.

47. A: The square root of the total number of data values. In a histogram, the number of bars is equal to the square root of the total number of data values. Histograms look like bar graphs, but the bars on a histogram represent the number of observations that fall within a particular range. Histograms are often used to locate multiple distributions or apply a distribution to capability analysis. The width of each bar in a histogram is calculated by dividing the range of data by the number of bars. The range of data is determined by subtracting the minimum data value from the maximum data value. On a histogram, the *x*-axis represents the data values of each bar, and the *y*-axis indicates the number of observations.

48. D: Normal. A normal distribution is appropriate for continuous data with neither an upper nor a lower boundary. Continuous data is obtained through measurement. A lognormal or Weibull distribution is appropriate for sets of continuous data with a fixed lower boundary but no upper boundary. In most lognormal and Weibull distributions, the lower boundary is zero. An exponential distribution is appropriate for continuous data sets in which the values are relatively consistent.

49. A: First-order main effects. In a contour plot, a series of evenly spaced parallel lines indicates first-order main effects. Interactions between responses are indicated by curving contour lines. Very few contour plots consist of evenly spaced parallel lines. The most general use of contour plots is during the improve stage of DMAIC, when they are used in response surface analysis to predict minimum and maximum response values for specific data ranges.

50. C: A known standard deviation. A known standard deviation increases the power of an estimation of the confidence interval on the mean. Indeed, when the standard deviation is known, the *z* tables may be used to find the confidence interval on the mean; when the standard deviation is unknown, the *t* tables must be used. The confidence interval on the mean is the percentage of samples that will contain the true population mean. It is assumed that the sample population will follow a normal distribution. When there are more samples, this increases the power of the estimation of the confidence interval on the mean.

How to Overcome Test Anxiety

Just the thought of taking a test is enough to make most people a little nervous. A test is an important event that can have a long-term impact on your future, so it's important to take it seriously and it's natural to feel anxious about performing well. But just because anxiety is normal, that doesn't mean that it's helpful in test taking, or that you should simply accept it as part of your life. Anxiety can have a variety of effects. These effects can be mild, like making you feel slightly nervous, or severe, like blocking your ability to focus or remember even a simple detail.

If you experience test anxiety—whether severe or mild—it's important to know how to beat it. To discover this, first you need to understand what causes test anxiety.

Causes of Test Anxiety

While we often think of anxiety as an uncontrollable emotional state, it can actually be caused by simple, practical things. One of the most common causes of test anxiety is that a person does not feel adequately prepared for their test. This feeling can be the result of many different issues such as poor study habits or lack of organization, but the most common culprit is time management. Starting to study too late, failing to organize your study time to cover all of the material, or being distracted while you study will mean that you're not well prepared for the test. This may lead to cramming the night before, which will cause you to be physically and mentally exhausted for the test. Poor time management also contributes to feelings of stress, fear, and hopelessness as you realize you are not well prepared but don't know what to do about it.

Other times, test anxiety is not related to your preparation for the test but comes from unresolved fear. This may be a past failure on a test, or poor performance on tests in general. It may come from comparing yourself to others who seem to be performing better or from the stress of living up to expectations. Anxiety may be driven by fears of the future—how failure on this test would affect your educational and career goals. These fears are often completely irrational, but they can still negatively impact your test performance.

Elements of Test Anxiety

As mentioned earlier, test anxiety is considered to be an emotional state, but it has physical and mental components as well. Sometimes you may not even realize that you are suffering from test anxiety until you notice the physical symptoms. These can include trembling hands, rapid heartbeat, sweating, nausea, and tense muscles. Extreme anxiety may lead to fainting or vomiting. Obviously, any of these symptoms can have a negative impact on testing. It is important to recognize them as soon as they begin to occur so that you can address the problem before it damages your performance.

The mental components of test anxiety include trouble focusing and inability to remember learned information. During a test, your mind is on high alert, which can help you recall information and stay focused for an extended period of time. However, anxiety interferes with your mind's natural processes, causing you to blank out, even on the questions you know well. The strain of testing during anxiety makes it difficult to stay focused, especially on a test that may take several hours. Extreme anxiety can take a huge mental toll, making it difficult not only to recall test information but even to understand the test questions or pull your thoughts together.

Effects of Test Anxiety

Test anxiety is like a disease—if left untreated, it will get progressively worse. Anxiety leads to poor performance, and this reinforces the feelings of fear and failure, which in turn lead to poor performances on subsequent tests. It can grow from a mild nervousness to a crippling condition. If allowed to progress, test anxiety can have a big impact on your schooling, and consequently on your future.

Test anxiety can spread to other parts of your life. Anxiety on tests can become anxiety in any stressful situation, and blanking on a test can turn into panicking in a job situation. But fortunately, you don't have to let anxiety rule your testing and determine your grades. There are a number of relatively simple steps you can take to move past anxiety and function normally on a test and in the rest of life.

Physical Steps for Beating Test Anxiety

While test anxiety is a serious problem, the good news is that it can be overcome. It doesn't have to control your ability to think and remember information. While it may take time, you can begin taking steps today to beat anxiety.

Just as your first hint that you may be struggling with anxiety comes from the physical symptoms, the first step to treating it is also physical. Rest is crucial for having a clear, strong mind. If you are tired, it is much easier to give in to anxiety. But if you establish good sleep habits, your body and mind will be ready to perform optimally, without the strain of exhaustion. Additionally, sleeping well helps you to retain information better, so you're more likely to recall the answers when you see the test questions.

Getting good sleep means more than going to bed on time. It's important to allow your brain time to relax. Take study breaks from time to time so it doesn't get overworked, and don't study right before bed. Take time to rest your mind before trying to rest your body, or you may find it difficult to fall asleep.

Along with sleep, other aspects of physical health are important in preparing for a test. Good nutrition is vital for good brain function. Sugary foods and drinks may give a burst of energy but this burst is followed by a crash, both physically and emotionally. Instead, fuel your body with protein and vitamin-rich foods.

Also, drink plenty of water. Dehydration can lead to headaches and exhaustion, especially if your brain is already under stress from the rigors of the test. Particularly if your test is a long one, drink water during the breaks. And if possible, take an energy-boosting snack to eat between sections.

Along with sleep and diet, a third important part of physical health is exercise. Maintaining a steady workout schedule is helpful, but even taking 5-minute study breaks to walk can help get your blood pumping faster and clear your head. Exercise also releases endorphins, which contribute to a positive feeling and can help combat test anxiety.

When you nurture your physical health, you are also contributing to your mental health. If your body is healthy, your mind is much more likely to be healthy as well. So take time to rest, nourish your body with healthy food and water, and get moving as much as possible. Taking these physical steps will make you stronger and more able to take the mental steps necessary to overcome test anxiety.

Mental Steps for Beating Test Anxiety

Working on the mental side of test anxiety can be more challenging, but as with the physical side, there are clear steps you can take to overcome it. As mentioned earlier, test anxiety often stems from lack of preparation, so the obvious solution is to prepare for the test. Effective studying may be the most important weapon you have for beating test anxiety, but you can and should employ several other mental tools to combat fear.

First, boost your confidence by reminding yourself of past success—tests or projects that you aced. If you're putting as much effort into preparing for this test as you did for those, there's no reason you should expect to fail here. Work hard to prepare; then trust your preparation.

Second, surround yourself with encouraging people. It can be helpful to find a study group, but be sure that the people you're around will encourage a positive attitude. If you spend time with others who are anxious or cynical, this will only contribute to your own anxiety. Look for others who are motivated to study hard from a desire to succeed, not from a fear of failure.

Third, reward yourself. A test is physically and mentally tiring, even without anxiety, and it can be helpful to have something to look forward to. Plan an activity following the test, regardless of the outcome, such as going to a movie or getting ice cream.

When you are taking the test, if you find yourself beginning to feel anxious, remind yourself that you know the material. Visualize successfully completing the test. Then take a few deep, relaxing breaths and return to it. Work through the questions carefully but with confidence, knowing that you are capable of succeeding.

Developing a healthy mental approach to test taking will also aid in other areas of life. Test anxiety affects more than just the actual test—it can be damaging to your mental health and even contribute to depression. It's important to beat test anxiety before it becomes a problem for more than testing.

Study Strategy

Being prepared for the test is necessary to combat anxiety, but what does being prepared look like? You may study for hours on end and still not feel prepared. What you need is a strategy for test prep. The next few pages outline our recommended steps to help you plan out and conquer the challenge of preparation.

Step 1: Scope Out the Test

Learn everything you can about the format (multiple choice, essay, etc.) and what will be on the test. Gather any study materials, course outlines, or sample exams that may be available. Not only will this help you to prepare, but knowing what to expect can help to alleviate test anxiety.

Step 2: Map Out the Material

Look through the textbook or study guide and make note of how many chapters or sections it has. Then divide these over the time you have. For example, if a book has 15 chapters and you have five days to study, you need to cover three chapters each day. Even better, if you have the time, leave an extra day at the end for overall review after you have gone through the material in depth.

If time is limited, you may need to prioritize the material. Look through it and make note of which sections you think you already have a good grasp on, and which need review. While you are studying, skim quickly through the familiar sections and take more time on the challenging parts.

Write out your plan so you don't get lost as you go. Having a written plan also helps you feel more in control of the study, so anxiety is less likely to arise from feeling overwhelmed at the amount to cover.

Step 3: Gather Your Tools

Decide what study method works best for you. Do you prefer to highlight in the book as you study and then go back over the highlighted portions? Or do you type out notes of the important information? Or is it helpful to make flashcards that you can carry with you? Assemble the pens, index cards, highlighters, post-it notes, and any other materials you may need so you won't be distracted by getting up to find things while you study.

If you're having a hard time retaining the information or organizing your notes, experiment with different methods. For example, try color-coding by subject with colored pens, highlighters, or post-it notes. If you learn better by hearing, try recording yourself reading your notes so you can listen while in the car, working out, or simply sitting at your desk. Ask a friend to quiz you from your flashcards, or try teaching someone the material to solidify it in your mind.

Step 4: Create Your Environment

It's important to avoid distractions while you study. This includes both the obvious distractions like visitors and the subtle distractions like an uncomfortable chair (or a too-comfortable couch that makes you want to fall asleep). Set up the best study environment possible: good lighting and a comfortable work area. If background music helps you focus, you may want to turn it on, but otherwise keep the room quiet. If you are using a computer to take notes, be sure you don't have any other windows open, especially applications like social media, games, or anything else that could distract you. Silence your phone and turn off notifications. Be sure to keep water close by so you stay hydrated while you study (but avoid unhealthy drinks and snacks).

Also, take into account the best time of day to study. Are you freshest first thing in the morning? Try to set aside some time then to work through the material. Is your mind clearer in the afternoon or evening? Schedule your study session then. Another method is to study at the same time of day that you will take the test, so that your brain gets used to working on the material at that time and will be ready to focus at test time.

Step 5: Study!

Once you have done all the study preparation, it's time to settle into the actual studying. Sit down, take a few moments to settle your mind so you can focus, and begin to follow your study plan. Don't give in to distractions or let yourself procrastinate. This is your time to prepare so you'll be ready to fearlessly approach the test. Make the most of the time and stay focused.

Of course, you don't want to burn out. If you study too long you may find that you're not retaining the information very well. Take regular study breaks. For example, taking five minutes out of every hour to walk briskly, breathing deeply and swinging your arms, can help your mind stay fresh.

As you get to the end of each chapter or section, it's a good idea to do a quick review. Remind yourself of what you learned and work on any difficult parts. When you feel that you've mastered the material, move on to the next part. At the end of your study session, briefly skim through your notes again.

But while review is helpful, cramming last minute is NOT. If at all possible, work ahead so that you won't need to fit all your study into the last day. Cramming overloads your brain with more information than it can process and retain, and your tired mind may struggle to recall even previously learned information when it is overwhelmed with last-minute study. Also, the urgent nature of cramming and the stress placed on your brain contribute to anxiety. You'll be more likely to go to the test feeling unprepared and having trouble thinking clearly.

So don't cram, and don't stay up late before the test, even just to review your notes at a leisurely pace. Your brain needs rest more than it needs to go over the information again. In fact, plan to finish your studies by noon or early afternoon the day before the test. Give your brain the rest of the day to relax or focus on other things, and get a good night's sleep. Then you will be fresh for the test and better able to recall what you've studied.

Step 6: Take a Practice Test

Many courses offer sample tests, either online or in the study materials. This is an excellent resource to check whether you have mastered the material, as well as to prepare for the test format and environment.

Check the test format ahead of time: the number of questions, the type (multiple choice, free response, etc.), and the time limit. Then create a plan for working through them. For example, if you have 30 minutes to take a 60-question test, your limit is 30 seconds per question. Spend less time on the questions you know well so that you can take more time on the difficult ones.

If you have time to take several practice tests, take the first one open book, with no time limit. Work through the questions at your own pace and make sure you fully understand them. Gradually work up to taking a test under test conditions: sit at a desk with all study materials put away and set a timer. Pace yourself to make sure you finish the test with time to spare and go back to check your answers if you have time.

After each test, check your answers. On the questions you missed, be sure you understand why you missed them. Did you misread the question (tests can use tricky wording)? Did you forget the information? Or was it something you hadn't learned? Go back and study any shaky areas that the practice tests reveal.

Taking these tests not only helps with your grade, but also aids in combating test anxiety. If you're already used to the test conditions, you're less likely to worry about it, and working through tests until you're scoring well gives you a confidence boost. Go through the practice tests until you feel comfortable, and then you can go into the test knowing that you're ready for it.

Test Tips

On test day, you should be confident, knowing that you've prepared well and are ready to answer the questions. But aside from preparation, there are several test day strategies you can employ to maximize your performance.

First, as stated before, get a good night's sleep the night before the test (and for several nights before that, if possible). Go into the test with a fresh, alert mind rather than staying up late to study.

Try not to change too much about your normal routine on the day of the test. It's important to eat a nutritious breakfast, but if you normally don't eat breakfast at all, consider eating just a protein bar. If you're a coffee drinker, go ahead and have your normal coffee. Just make sure you time it so that the caffeine doesn't wear off right in the middle of your test. Avoid sugary beverages, and drink enough water to stay hydrated but not so much that you need a restroom break 10 minutes into the test. If your test isn't first thing in the morning, consider going for a walk or doing a light workout before the test to get your blood flowing.

Allow yourself enough time to get ready, and leave for the test with plenty of time to spare so you won't have the anxiety of scrambling to arrive in time. Another reason to be early is to select a good seat. It's helpful to sit away from doors and windows, which can be distracting. Find a good seat, get out your supplies, and settle your mind before the test begins.

When the test begins, start by going over the instructions carefully, even if you already know what to expect. Make sure you avoid any careless mistakes by following the directions.

Then begin working through the questions, pacing yourself as you've practiced. If you're not sure on an answer, don't spend too much time on it, and don't let it shake your confidence. Either skip it and come back later, or eliminate as many wrong answers as possible and guess among the remaining ones. Don't dwell on these questions as you continue—put them out of your mind and focus on what lies ahead.

Be sure to read all of the answer choices, even if you're sure the first one is the right answer. Sometimes you'll find a better one if you keep reading. But don't second-guess yourself if you do immediately know the answer. Your gut instinct is usually right. Don't let test anxiety rob you of the information you know.

If you have time at the end of the test (and if the test format allows), go back and review your answers. Be cautious about changing any, since your first instinct tends to be correct, but make sure you didn't misread any of the questions or accidentally mark the wrong answer choice. Look over any you skipped and make an educated guess.

At the end, leave the test feeling confident. You've done your best, so don't waste time worrying about your performance or wishing you could change anything. Instead, celebrate the successful completion of this test. And finally, use this test to learn how to deal with anxiety even better next time.

Review Video: Test Anxiety
Visit mometrix.com/academy and enter code: 100340

Important Qualification

Not all anxiety is created equal. If your test anxiety is causing major issues in your life beyond the classroom or testing center, or if you are experiencing troubling physical symptoms related to your anxiety, it may be a sign of a serious physiological or psychological condition. If this sounds like your situation, we strongly encourage you to seek professional help.

Online Resources

Due to our efforts to try to keep this book to a manageable length, we've created a link that will give you access to all of your online resources:

mometrix.com/resources719/sixsigmayb

It's Your Moment, Let's Celebrate It!

Share your story @mometrixtestpreparation